Being a Writer™

Funding for Developmental Studies Center has been generously provided by:

The Annenberg Foundation, Inc.

The Atlantic Philanthropies (USA) Inc.

Booth Ferris Foundation

The Robert Bowne Foundation, Inc.

The Annie E. Casey Foundation

Center for Substance Abuse Prevention
    U.S. Department of Health and Human Services

The Danforth Foundation

The DuBarry Foundation

The Ford Foundation

Google Inc.

William T. Grant Foundation

Evelyn and Walter Haas, Jr. Fund

Walter and Elise Haas Fund

The Horace Hagedorn Foundation

J. David and Pamela Hakman Family Foundation

Hasbro Children's Foundation

Charles Hayden Foundation

The William Randolph Hearst Foundations

Clarence E. Heller Charitable Foundation

The William and Flora Hewlett Foundation

The James Irvine Foundation

The Robert Wood Johnson Foundation

Walter S. Johnson Foundation

Ewing Marion Kauffman Foundation

W.K. Kellogg Foundation

John S. and James L. Knight Foundation

Lilly Endowment, Inc.

Longview Foundation

Louis R. Lurie Foundation

The John D. and Catherine T. MacArthur Foundation

A.L. Mailman Family Foundation, Inc.

The MBK Foundation

Mr. and Mrs. Sanford N. McDonnell

Mendelson Family Fund

MetLife Foundation

Charles Stewart Mott Foundation

National Institute on Drug Abuse,
    National Institutes of Health

National Science Foundation

New York Life Foundation

Nippon Life Insurance Foundation

Karen and Christopher Payne Foundation

The Pew Charitable Trusts

The Pinkerton Foundation

The Rockefeller Foundation

Louise and Claude Rosenberg, Jr. Family Foundation

The San Francisco Foundation

Shinnyo-en Foundation

Silver Giving Foundation

The Spencer Foundation

Spunk Fund, Inc.

Stephen Bechtel Fund

W. Clement and Jessie V. Stone Foundation

Stuart Foundation

The Stupski Family Foundation

The Sulzberger Foundation, Inc.

Surdna Foundation, Inc.

John Templeton Foundation

U.S. Department of Education

The Wallace Foundation

Wells Fargo Bank

Grade 3

Being a Writer™

**DEVELOPMENTAL
STUDIES CENTER**™

First edition published 2007.

Being a Writer is a trademark of Developmental Studies Center.

Developmental Studies Center wishes to thank the following authors, agents, and publishers for their permission to reprint materials included in this program. Many people went out of their way to help us secure these rights and we are very grateful for their support. Every effort has been made to trace the ownership of copyrighted material and to make full acknowledgment of its use. If errors or omissions have occurred, they will be corrected in subsequent editions, provided that notification is submitted in writing to the publisher.

"Joanne Ryder" reprinted by permission from *The Big Book of Picture-Book Authors and Illustrators* by James Preller. Scholastic Inc./Teaching Resources. Copyright © 2001 by James Preller. Excerpt from *Reptiles: A True Book by Melissa Stewart*. Copyright © 2001 by Melissa Stewart. All rights reserved. Reprinted by permission of Children's Press, an imprint of Scholastic Library Publishing, Inc. Excerpt from *Where Butterflies Grow* by Joanne Ryder, copyright © 1989 by Joanne Ryder. Used by permission of Lodestar Books, an affiliate of Dutton Children's Books, A Division of Penguin Young Readers Group, A Member of Penguin Group (USA) Inc., 345 Hudson Street, New York, NY 10014. All rights reserved. Excerpt from *Into the Sea* by Brenda Z. Guiberson © 1996 by Brenda Z. Guiberson. Reprinted by permission of Henry Holt and Company, LLC.

A special thanks to Donald Murray (who passed away December 30, 2006) for the wonderful assortment of author quotations that he gathered in his book *shoptalk: learning to write* published by Boynton/Cook Publishers in 1990.

Developmental Studies Center
2000 Embarcadero, Suite 305
Oakland, CA 94606-5300
(800) 666-7270, fax: (510) 464-3670
www.devstu.org

ISBN: 978-1-59892-317-9

Printed in the United States of America

 4 5 6 7 8 9 10 MLY 16 15 14 13 12

TABLE OF CONTENTS

Genre Expository Nonfiction 373
    Week 1 376
    Week 2 396
    Week 3 417
    Week 4 435
    Week 5 455
    Week 6 473

Genre Functional Writing 491
    Week 1 494
    Week 2 515
    Week 3 533

Unit 7 Revisiting the Writing Community 549
    Week 1 551

Skill Development Chart 568

Bibliography 569

Blackline Masters 573

Expository Nonfiction

Genre

Expository Nonfiction

Genre Expository Nonfiction

During this six-week unit, the students immerse themselves in nonfiction text about animals and then select one of those animals to research with a partner in some depth. Partners then write, revise, and publish an informational piece about the animal to share with the class. They learn research skills such as taking notes and categorizing, and they learn about features of expository text. Partners learn to share resources fairly, make decisions together, and take responsibility for their own part of the work.

Development Across the Grades

Grade	Nonfiction Topics and Genre	Research Skills	Writing Skills and Conventions
3	• Select an **animal** to research and write about • Q&A, ABC, and other formats for nonfiction • Tables of contents, illustrations, and captions	• Pre-research writing • Generating questions • Taking notes • Organizing information by subtopic	• Commas in a series • Apostrophes to show possession • Listening for periods
4	• Select a **country** to research and write about • Q&A, pattern, and other formats for nonfiction • Maps and diagrams	• Pre-research writing • Narrowing research focus • Taking notes • Organizing information by subtopic	• Various uses of commas • Capitalizing languages, religions, and holidays • Listening for periods
5	• Select **any nonfiction topic** to research and write about • Explore different ways to communicate information • Sidebars and glossaries	• Pre-research writing • Narrowing research focus • Taking notes and organizing information by subtopic	• Transition words (conjunctions) • Citing resources • Listening for periods
6	• Select **any nonfiction topic** to research and write about • Explore different ways to communicate information • Introductions and indexes	• Pre-research writing • Narrowing research focus • Taking notes and organizing information by subtopic	• Transition words (conjunctions) • Citing resources • Paragraphing • First, second, and third person points of view

UNIT OVERVIEW

WEEK	DAY 1	DAY 2	DAY 3	DAY 4
	Immersion and Topic Exploration			
1	**Exploring Nonfiction:** *Have You Seen Bugs?* **Focus:** Animal topics	**Exploring Nonfiction:** *A Pack of Wolves* **Quick-Write:** Questions about animals	**Exploring Nonfiction:** *Reptiles* **Focus:** Chapter headings as subtopics	**Exploring Nonfiction:** *The Furry Animal Alphabet Book* **Focus:** Alphabet books
2	**Exploring Nonfiction:** *Into the Sea* **Focus:** Following one individual	**Exploring Nonfiction:** *Little Panda* **Focus:** Photographs in nonfiction	**Exploring Nonfiction:** *Where Butterflies Grow* **Quick-Write:** An animal's point of view	**Meeting an Author and Pair Conferring** **Focus:** Joanne Ryder; list animals and narrow choices
	Topic Selection, Research, and Drafting			
3	**Selecting Topics** **Focus:** Selecting an animal to research; preresearch writing	**Selecting Topics** **Focus:** Generating research questions	**Researching and Taking Notes** **Focus:** Taking notes	**Researching and Taking Notes** **Focus:** Taking notes
4	**Researching and Taking Notes** **Focus:** Reviewing and adding to notes	**Organizing Notes** **Focus:** Organizing notes and researching further where necessary	**Drafting and Pair Conferring** **Focus:** Drafting	**Drafting and Pair Conferring** **Focus:** Drafting
	Revision, Proofreading, and Publication			
5	**Drafting and Pair Conferring** **Focus:** Illustrations and captions	**Analyzing and Revising Drafts** **Quick-Write:** Strong opening sentences	**Analyzing and Revising Drafts** **Focus:** Checking for order, interest, completeness	**Group Conferring** **Focus:** Does it all make sense?
6	**Writing Final Versions** **Focus:** Table of contents	**Writing Final Versions and Proofreading** **Focus:** Spelling and punctuation	**Writing Final Versions and Publishing** **Focus:** Author's Chair sharing	**Writing Final Versions and Publishing** **Focus:** Author's Chair sharing

Week 1 Overview

GENRE: EXPOSITORY NONFICTION

Have You Seen Bugs?
by Joanne Oppenheim, illustrated by Ron Broda
(Scholastic, Inc., 1999)

Bugs of all kinds are described in poetic language.

A Pack of Wolves
by Richard and Louise Spilsbury (Heinemann, 2003)

Life in a wolf pack is described in detail.

Reptiles
by Melissa Stewart (Children's Press, 2001)

This book tells all about reptiles, from crocodiles to slithery snakes.

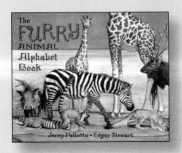

The Furry Animal Alphabet Book
by Jerry Pallotta, illustrated by Edgar Stewart (Charlesbridge, 1991)

Mammals exotic and ordinary are described in an alphabet format.

Writing Focus

- Students hear and discuss expository nonfiction.

- Students explore different ways to organize and present information in nonfiction.

- Students begin reading and writing about animals that interest them.

- Students cultivate curiosity about nonfiction topics related to animals.

Social Focus

- Students act in fair and caring ways.

- Students make decisions and solve problems respectfully.

DO AHEAD

- Prior to Day 1, decide how you will randomly assign partners to work together during the unit. See the front matter for suggestions about assigning partners randomly (see page xiii) and for considerations for pairing English Language Learners (see page xxviii).

- Consider prereading this week's read-aloud selections with your English Language Learners. Show and discuss illustrations in the books. Stop during the reading to discuss vocabulary and to check for understanding. (See ELL vocabulary listed in the lessons.)

- Prior to Day 3, collect nonfiction books, magazine articles, and other written materials on a variety of animals. Select texts that are informational (expository) in nature and that represent a variety of nonfiction styles.

"Curiosity urges you on—the driving force."
    — John Dos Passos

Nonfiction writers aren't necessarily experts on the topics they write about, but they are curious and ask themselves questions, conduct research, and communicate what they learn in an interesting way.

In this unit, the students learn and write about animals that interest them. List animals you are curious about, followed by some things you are curious to know about them. Ask yourself:

- What is amazing to you about animals?

- What is the most unusual creature you've ever seen up close? Describe the experience.

- If you could be an animal for a day, what would you be? Why?

Day 1

Materials

- *Have You Seen Bugs?*
- *Oceans and Seas* from Unit 1
- *Atlantic* from Unit 1
- *I Wonder Why the Sea Is Salty* from Unit 1
- Chart paper and a marker

Exploring Nonfiction

In this lesson, the students:

- Work with a new partner
- Hear and discuss expository nonfiction
- Explore how information is organized and presented
- Explore and write about animals that interest them

About Teaching Nonfiction Writing

There are three phases to the nonfiction unit in grade 3: Immersion and Topic Exploration; Topic Selection, Research, and Drafting; and Revision, Proofreading, and Publication. During each two-week phase, the students learn about interesting ways that information can be organized and presented in nonfiction, while letting their curiosity lead their exploration about animals.

In Weeks 1 and 2, the students read many nonfiction resources about animals and write short pieces about what they are learning. This process prepares them to select, in pairs, one animal to research and write about. During Weeks 3 and 4, pairs research their chosen animal and begin drafting their informational nonfiction pieces. The last two weeks of the unit are spent exploring nonfiction craft and conventions and integrating these as appropriate into their final drafts.

GETTING READY TO WRITE

▶1 Pair Students and Discuss Working Together

Teacher Note ▶

The partners you assign today will stay together for the unit.

Making Meaning® Teacher

You can either have the students work with their current *Making Meaning* partner or assign them a new partner for this unit.

Randomly assign partners (see "Do Ahead" on page 377) and make sure they know each other's names. Gather the class with partners sitting together, facing you. Have them bring their writing notebooks and pencils.

Explain that over the next six weeks partners will work together to explore writing nonfiction. They will hear and discuss interesting nonfiction books and write about topics that interest them.

Have partners take a couple of minutes to get to know each other by talking about some of the things they have written so far this year; then signal for their attention and ask:

Q *What did you learn about the writing your partner has done this year?*

2 ▶ Introduce Nonfiction

Show the covers of *Oceans and Seas*, *Atlantic*, and *I Wonder Why the Sea Is Salty*. Remind the students that they heard these examples of nonfiction earlier in the year. Ask and briefly discuss:

Q *What do you think you know about nonfiction?*

Students might say:

"Nonfiction is real. It's about true things."

"I agree with [Elias] because you can learn facts from nonfiction."

"It's not a made-up story."

"In addition to what [Wendy] said, it can be about science, like animals or planets."

Point out that nonfiction writers write about real things that they are curious about. They write about these topics in a way that helps readers become interested in and curious about them, too. Explain that in the coming weeks the students will hear different examples of nonfiction to help them get ideas for their own nonfiction writing.

3 ▶ Read *Have You Seen Bugs?* Aloud

Show the cover of *Have You Seen Bugs?* and read the title and the author's and illustrator's names aloud. Explain that you will read the book aloud, and invite the students to think about what kinds of information the author gives about bugs in this book.

Read the book aloud slowly and clearly, showing the illustrations and clarifying vocabulary as you read.

◀ **Teacher Note**

If necessary, remind the students to use the discussion prompts to connect their ideas to those of others. The prompts are:

- "I agree with _____ because…"
- "I disagree with _____ because…"
- "In addition to what _____ said, I think…"

◀ **Teacher Note**

The students will be familiar with *Have You Seen Bugs?* as it was read aloud in *Making Meaning* Unit 2, Week 1. Tell the students that they will listen to it again, this time thinking about how the author wrote the book.

Teacher Note

To review the procedure for defining vocabulary during the read-aloud, see volume 1, page 45.

Suggested Vocabulary

iridescent: having rainbowlike colors (p. 4)

thickets: plants or shrubs growing close together (p. 16)

chrysalis: cocoon (p. 25)

antennae: long, thin growths on an insect's head (p. 18)

ELL Vocabulary

English Language Learners may benefit from discussing additional vocabulary, including:

speckles: spots (p. 2)

burrowed: dug into (p. 6)

cocoon: a covering spun by some bugs to protect their growing eggs or babies (p. 25)

seldom at rest: hardly ever resting (p. 28)

billions: a very, very large number (p. 30)

4 ▶ Discuss the Story and Generate Animal Topics

Ask and briefly discuss:

Q   *What is something you found out about bugs?*

Point out that in this book the author asks readers questions to help us think about bugs. Show and reread the questions that appear on pages 1, 10, 16, 20, 22, and 26.

Use "Think, Pair, Share" to have the students first think about and then discuss:

Teacher Note ▶

To review the procedure for "Think, Pair, Share," see volume 1, page xiv.

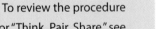 **Q**   *If you were going to write an animal book like this one, called* Have You Seen _____, *what animal might you write about, and why?* [pause] *Turn to your partner.*

After partners have talked, have a few volunteers share their thinking with the class. Record their ideas on a sheet of chart paper entitled "Have You Seen _____?"

Students might say:

"I would write a book called *Have You Seen Dogs?* because I love dogs."

"I would write *Have You Seen Fish?* because when I went to the aquarium with my cousin I saw lots of different fish."

"It would write *Have You Seen Cheetahs?* because cheetahs are my favorite animal."

▶ Review Nonfiction Topics in Writing Notebooks

Ask the students to open to the writing ideas section of their writing notebooks and review the nonfiction topics they have listed so far this year. Ask and briefly discuss:

Q   *Which nonfiction topics have you written about so far this year?*

Q   *Which of your nonfiction topics are about animals?*

Have the students put a star next to any topics on their lists that are related to animals.

Explain that during writing time today the students may add animal topics to their writing ideas section, think of more ideas for a *Have You Seen?* book, or write about anything else they choose. Make *Have You Seen Bugs?* available for interested students to look at if they wish.

WRITING TIME

Write Independently

Ask the students to return to their seats. Write the following choices on the board and have them write silently for 20–30 minutes.

* Add animal topics to your writing ideas section.

* Think of other ideas for a *Have You Seen?* book.

* Write about anything you choose.

If necessary, remind the students to double-space their writing. Also review that during the silent writing period there should be no

◀ **Teacher Note**

If the students have difficulty generating ideas, stimulate their thinking by suggesting some of the ideas in the "Students might say" note. Then ask, "What other animals might you write about?"

◀ **Teacher Note**

Note that on Days 1 and 2 of the unit, the students may write nonfiction or anything else they choose. On Day 3, after exposure to a couple more examples of nonfiction, they will all begin writing in this genre.

talking, whispering, or walking around. Join the students in writing for a few minutes; then walk around the room and observe.

Signal to let the students know when writing time is over.

SHARING AND REFLECTING

▶7 Share Writing and Reflect

Gather the class with partners sitting together, facing you. Ask partners to briefly tell each other what they wrote about today. Encourage them to listen carefully, as they will be responsible for sharing what their partner wrote about with the class.

After a moment, signal for their attention and ask:

Q *What did your partner write about today?*

Q *What did you and your new partner do to work well together when talking and sharing your writing?*

ELL Note

You might provide the prompt "My partner wrote about…" to your English Language Learners to help them verbalize their answers to this question.

EXTENSION

Explore Poetry About Nonfiction Topics

Point out that the author of *Have You Seen Bugs?* chose to communicate information about bugs using rhyme, making this book poetry as well as nonfiction. Reread parts of the book, inviting the students to listen to the rhyming patterns. Consider finding and reading other poems that give factual information about nonfiction topics, such as *Have You Seen Birds?* also by Joanne Oppenheimer and numerous titles by Ruth Heller, including *Chickens Aren't the Only Ones*, *Plants That Never Bloom*, and *How to Hide a Butterfly*.

Day 2

Exploring Nonfiction

In this lesson, the students:

* Hear and discuss expository nonfiction
* Explore how information is organized and presented
* List questions they could ask about animals
* Cultivate curiosity

About Cultivating Curiosity as a Writer

Curiosity is an important quality for students to cultivate, both as readers and budding writers of nonfiction. We want them to learn that they do not need to know everything about a topic before they start writing about it; it is enough to be curious about it and know how to go about finding information. Writing is a process of discovering that there is information that we don't know, finding out about it, and communicating about it in a way that informs and/or makes others curious, too.

This is a good time of year to schedule field trips to stimulate the students' curiosity about topics that they can then research back in the classroom. Consider taking the students to science museums, zoos, aquariums, and natural settings such as parks or creeks.

GETTING READY TO WRITE

▶1 Discuss Curiosity

Gather the class with partners sitting together, facing you. Review that yesterday the students began exploring nonfiction. They heard *Have You Seen Bugs?* and started thinking about animals they are curious about. Ask and briefly discuss:

Q *Why might curiosity be an important quality for a writer to have?*

Students might say:

"It's good for writers to be curious so they can find out lots of interesting things and write about them."

"If writers aren't curious, they won't get interested in anything to write about."

Materials

* *A Pack of Wolves*

 Note

If necessary, define *curiosity* as "a wish to know more about something."

Explain that writers don't have to know a lot about a topic when they begin writing about it, but they do need to be curious about it. By researching things they wonder about, writers gather interesting information that they can share with others in their writing.

Explain that today the students will hear a nonfiction book that is also about the animal kingdom but written in a style different from *Have You Seen Bugs?*

▶2 Read and Discuss Parts of *A Pack of Wolves*

Show the cover of *A Pack of Wolves* and read the title and authors' names aloud. Invite the students to think as they listen about how the authors chose to present the information about wolves in this book.

Show the table of contents on page 3 and explain that the "Contents" page lists the names of the chapters, along with the page numbers where they begin. Read the chapter titles aloud and then explain that you will read the first three chapters aloud.

Read pages 4–8 aloud, showing the illustrations and reading the captions. Ask and briefly discuss:

Q   *What interesting things have you heard so far about wolves?*

Q   *What are you curious about?*

Q   *How do the authors present the information about wolves in this book?*

Teacher Note   ▶

If the students have difficulty reporting things they are curious about, mention one or two things you are curious about and then ask the question again.

If necessary, point out that the authors use a question-and-answer format to give the information about wolves. As a class, select two or three more questions on the "Contents" page and read those chapters aloud. (If the chapter is long, consider reading just part of it.)

Point out that the authors use a question-and-answer format throughout the book to give information about wolves. Read several more questions from the table of contents aloud and select a couple of questions as a class. Read the answers aloud.

Quick-Write: Brainstorm Questions About an Animal

Ask the students to think of an animal they are curious about. They may review their nonfiction topics in the writing ideas section of their notebooks, if they wish. Have them open to the next blank page in their writing notebooks and write the name of that animal at the top of the page. Ask them to think quietly for a moment about:

Q *If you were going to write a question-and-answer book about the animal you chose, what questions could you write?*

Have the students take 5 minutes to jot down their questions; then have them discuss their topics and questions in pairs. Signal for their attention and have them write any additional questions they thought of while they were talking. Have a few volunteers share their animal and some of their questions with the class.

Explain that during writing time today the students may write more questions about the animal they chose, questions about other animals that interest them, or anything else they choose. Make *A Pack of Wolves* available for interested students to look at if they wish.

 Note

If necessary, rephrase this question in the following way:

Q *What animal do you want to know more about?*

Q *What do you want to know about that animal? How can you write that as a question?*

WRITING TIME

 ## Write Independently

Ask the students to return to their seats. Write the following choices on the board and have them write silently for 20–30 minutes.

- Write more questions about the animal you chose.

- Write questions about other animals.

- Write about anything you choose.

Join the students in writing for a few minutes; then walk around the room and observe.

Signal to let the students know when writing time is over.

SHARING AND REFLECTING

 Briefly Share Writing and Reflect on Curiosity

Ask partners to talk briefly about what they wrote about today. Ask them to be ready to share with the class what their partner wrote about.

After a moment, signal for their attention and ask:

Q *What did your partner write about today? What makes you curious about what your partner wrote?*

Have a few volunteers share with the class.

Day 3

Exploring Nonfiction

In this lesson, the students:

- Hear, read, and discuss expository nonfiction about animals
- Explore how information is organized and presented
- Write about what they learned and what they are curious about
- Share materials fairly
- Discuss and solve problems that arise in their work together

GETTING READY TO WRITE

1 ▶ Briefly Review Nonfiction Writing

Gather the class with partners sitting together, facing you. Review that the students heard text from two nonfiction books this week, *Have You Seen Bugs?* and *A Pack of Wolves*. Point out that in both books the authors used questions to communicate information.

On a sheet of chart paper entitled "Ways to Present Nonfiction Information," write *questions and answers*. Explain that you will continue to record different ways nonfiction authors organize and present information as you read aloud in the coming days.

Explain that today the students will hear a book about another type of animal. Invite them to think about how this book presents information in a way similar to or different from the other two books.

2 ▶ Read and Discuss Parts of *Reptiles*

Show the cover of *Reptiles* and read the title and author's name aloud. As you did on Day 2, show and read the "Contents" page (page 3) aloud.

Materials

- *Reptiles*
- Chart paper and a marker
- Collected nonfiction texts about animals (see "Do Ahead" on page 377)
- *Assessment Resource Book*

Making Meaning® Teacher

Your students may be familiar with *Reptiles*, as it is used in *Making Meaning* Grade 3, Unit 5, Week 3. If so, tell them that they will hear just part of the book reread today and that this time they will explore the book as a writer, rather than as a reader.

Explain that you will read a few of the chapters aloud. Read pages 10–20 slowly and clearly. Point out the "Important Words" page at the back of the book (page 46). Use this page to find and read aloud the meaning of *Jacobson's organ* (page 13).

ELL Vocabulary

English Language Learners may benefit from discussing the following vocabulary:

continent: one of seven groups of countries that make up the world (p. 14)

predators: animals that kill other animals for food (p. 18)

surroundings: the area where something lives (p. 19)

Ask and briefly discuss:

Q *How is this book organized [similarly to/differently from] A Pack of Wolves?*

Point out that *Reptiles* is similar to *A Pack of Wolves* in that it has chapters, but it is different in that the chapter titles are the names of different topics rather than questions (except for the first chapter).

 Discuss Nonfiction Resources

Explain that the students have now heard three books about animals and that they will have a chance to learn and write about different animals as well. Later in this unit, they will select an animal to research in detail, write about it, and then share their writing with the class. To prepare, they will spend the rest of this week and the next week exploring different animals they are curious about.

Emphasize that the students should not become attached to any particular animal at this point. The goal for the next week is to explore many different animals rather than any one animal in depth.

Direct the students' attention to the animal books and materials you have collected. Explain that they may explore these resources, as well as any others they might find (at the library, on the Internet, etc.) about animals of interest to them. Explain that the students will need to share these resources over coming weeks, and ask:

Q *What will we need to do to share these books and materials fairly?*

Q *If someone is reading a book you want to look at, what can you do?*

Q *If you are reading a book someone else is interested in, what can you do to share it fairly?*

Encourage the students to try the things they suggested for sharing the materials fairly. Tell them you will check in with them at the end of the lesson to see how they did.

◀ Explain how you will distribute the materials and have the students return to their seats.

WRITING TIME

 ### Read Nonfiction Texts

Have the students spend 15–20 minutes browsing the nonfiction materials and reading about animals they are curious about. Interested students might visit the school library or search the Internet during this period. Be ready to assist students in thinking about animals they are interested in and finding information about them.

 ### Write About What They Read

Call for the students' attention and have them close their books and other materials. Use "Think, Pair, Share" to have partners first think about and then discuss:

 Q *What did you find out from your reading today, and what are you curious about?* [pause] *Turn to your partner.*

After partners have shared, have several volunteers share their thinking with the class.

> ***Students might say:***
>
> "I read about pandas. I found out that pandas eat bamboo. I'm curious to find out if they eat anything else."
>
> "I read about owls. I found out that owls can turn their heads almost all the way around. I wonder what other animals can do that."

Teacher Note

Some options for distributing the nonfiction books and materials:

- While the class is still gathered, say some of the animal topics aloud and hand books to students who show interest in those animals.

- Lay materials out on a table and call groups to come and browse.

- Expand the nonfiction area of the class library and invite students to browse and help themselves.

- Place a selection of materials in several baskets and rotate the baskets among groups over the coming days.

 Note

Consider searching for resources about animals written in your students' native languages.

Teacher Note ▶

Note that the writing time is shortened for a few days to accommodate the reading of nonfiction texts.

Have the students open their writing notebooks to the next blank page. Write the following tasks on the board and have them work silently for 10–15 minutes.

● Write one or two interesting things you found out about an animal today.

● Write one or two things you are curious about.

● Add any new topics that interest you in the writing ideas section.

As the students write, walk around and observe.

CLASS ASSESSMENT NOTE

Observe the students and ask yourself:

● Are the students able to write about things they've learned or are curious about?

If you notice many students struggling to write, call for their attention and model writing as a class. Call on a volunteer to report what she read about, interesting things she learned, and things she is curious about. Record this information where everyone can see it. (For example, *I was curious about aardvarks. I found out that aardvarks are nocturnal animals. That means that they are awake at night and they sleep during the day. I learned that aardvarks use their strong front legs to dig out ants and termites to eat.*) After modeling, have the students resume writing on their own for a few more minutes.

Record your observations in the *Assessment Resource Book*.

Signal to let the students know when writing time is over. Explain that they will continue to explore animals in the coming days.

Ask the students to return the nonfiction materials they read today so others can read them tomorrow. Remind them not to become attached to any particular book or animal at this point; they will explore many different animals before choosing one to explore in depth.

SHARING AND REFLECTING

 Reflect on Sharing Materials Fairly

Ask and briefly discuss:

Q *What did you do to share the books and materials fairly today?*

Q *What problems did you have sharing the materials? What can we do tomorrow to avoid those problems?*

Students might say:

"I was waiting to look at the book about penguins, but the person who was reading it gave it to someone else when she was done."

"Maybe we could put a self-stick note on the front of the book with the names of the people who want to look at it."

"I agree with [Ron]. Then we can just pass the book to the next person on the list."

"In addition to what [Ron] said, I think we should try not to take too long with a book if we know other people want to see it."

Explain that you will remind the students about their proposed solutions before they browse nonfiction books again tomorrow.

Teacher Note

Save the "Ways to Present Nonfiction Information" chart to use on Day 4.

Day 4

Materials

- *The Furry Animal Alphabet Book*
- *Reptiles* from Day 3
- "Ways to Present Nonfiction Information" chart from Day 3
- Collected nonfiction texts
- A marker

Exploring Nonfiction

In this lesson, the students:

- Hear, read, and discuss expository nonfiction about animals
- Write about what they learned and what they are curious about
- Share materials fairly
- Assess how a solution is working and modify it if necessary

GETTING READY TO WRITE

 Briefly Review

Gather the class with partners sitting together, facing you. Direct their attention to the "Ways to Present Nonfiction Information" chart and review that the chart shows different ways authors can organize information when writing nonfiction. Show the cover and a few pages from *Reptiles*. Ask:

Q *How is information presented in* Reptiles?

If necessary, remind the students that information in *Reptiles* is organized into chapters by topics, such as type of reptile. On the chart, write *chapters about different topics*.

Explain that the students will hear another nonfiction book containing animal facts today. Encourage them to pay attention to the way information is presented in the book.

Read and Discuss Parts of *The Furry Animal Alphabet Book*

Show the cover of *The Furry Animal Alphabet Book* and read the title and author's name aloud. Ask:

Q *What are some animals that might be included in this book? What makes you think that?*

Explain that you will read a few of the pages aloud. Encourage the students to think about what they are curious about as they listen.

Read the text for the letters A, B, C, and D aloud, showing the illustrations and clarifying vocabulary as you read. Show a sampling of the subsequent pages but do not read them. Read the text for the letters X, Y, and Z aloud.

Suggested Vocabulary

aquatic: having to do with water (page for "Y")

marsupial: type of animal in which females have a pouch for their babies (page for "Y")

ELL Vocabulary

English Language Learners may benefit from discussing additional vocabulary, including:

gnaw: bite on (page for "B")

blur: something that is hard to see (page for "C")

zillion: a made-up word for a very large number (page for "Z")

Ask and briefly discuss:

Q *How is the information about animals presented in this book?*

If necessary, point out that the author uses the alphabet to organize information about furry animals. Add *alphabet books* to the "Ways to Present Nonfiction Information" chart.

Explain that during writing time today, the students will continue to read about and explore animals they are curious about. Encourage them to notice how information is organized as they read. Remind them of your expectations regarding handling of collected materials.

Also remind them of any solutions they proposed yesterday for sharing the materials more fairly. Tell them you will check in with them later to see how they did.

Have the students return to their seats. Make *The Furry Animal Alphabet Book* available for the students to look at, if they wish.

WRITING TIME

3 ▶ Read Nonfiction Texts

Teacher Note ▶

As the students work, ask individuals what they notice about how information is organized in the sources they are reading.

Have the students spend 15–20 minutes browsing the nonfiction materials and reading about animals they are curious about. Interested students might visit the school library or search the Internet. Be ready to assist students in thinking of animals and finding information about them.

4 ▶ Write About What They Read

Call for the students' attention and have them close their books and other materials. Ask and briefly discuss:

Q *When reading today, what did you notice about how the information you looked at is organized?*

 Q *What did you find out from your reading today and what are you curious about?* [pause] *Turn to your partner.*

Have the students open their writing notebooks to the next blank page. Write the following tasks on the board and have them work silently for 10–15 minutes.

● Write one or two interesting things you found out about an animal today.

● Write one or two things you are curious about.

● Add any new topics that interest you in the writing ideas section.

As the students write, walk around and observe. Signal to let the students know when writing time is over.

SHARING AND REFLECTING

 Reflect on Writing

Invite interested students to read aloud what they wrote today in their notebooks. Ask and briefly discuss:

Q   *What did you hear your classmates share that makes you curious?*

Q   *What did you do to share the materials fairly today? How did that work?*

Q   *What problems, if any, are we still having with sharing materials fairly? What else can we do to avoid those problems next time?*

Teacher Note

Save the "Ways to Present Nonfiction Information" chart to use in Week 2 and throughout the unit.

EXTENSION

Find Information About Animals

Invite the students to learn more online about animals they are curious about. Some relevant websites include: http://nationalzoo.si.edu, http://animal.discovery.com, and www.enature.com/fieldguides. Other websites can be found by searching by animal names.

Week 2 Overview

GENRE: EXPOSITORY NONFICTION

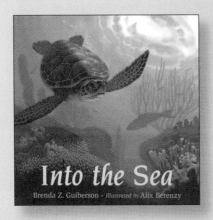

Into the Sea
by Brenda Z. Guiberson
(Henry Holt and Company, 1996)

Follow a turtle through its life cycle.

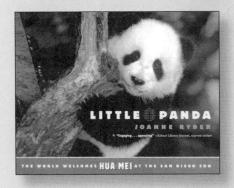

Little Panda
by Joanne Ryder
(Aladdin, 2001)

This book chronicles panda Hua Mei's first year at the San Diego Zoo.

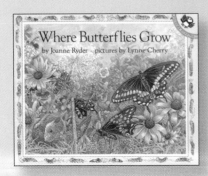

Where Butterflies Grow
by Joanne Ryder
(Puffin Books, 1989)

Experience a garden from a bug's point of view.

Writing Focus

- Students hear and discuss expository nonfiction.

- Students think about different ways to organize and present information in nonfiction.

- Students learn about a professional author's writing practice.

- Students read and write about animals that interest them.

- Students cultivate and express curiosity.

Social Focus

- Students act in fair and caring ways.

- Students make decisions and solve problems respectfully.

- Students express interest in and appreciation for one another's writing.

DO AHEAD

- Consider prereading this week's read-aloud selections with your English Language Learners. Show and discuss illustrations in the books. Stop during the reading to discuss vocabulary and to check for understanding. (See ELL vocabulary given in each lesson.)

TEACHER AS WRITER

"Writing is like exploring…. As an explorer makes maps of the country he has explored, so a writer's works are maps of the country he has explored."
— Lawrence Osgood

Choose one of the animals you listed last week that you are curious about and write its name at the top of a blank page in your notebook. Below the name of the animal, write five questions you have about that animal and five places you could go to look for answers. For example:

Topic: Dolphins

- Are they really as smart as people think?

- Do they mate for life?

- How have humans interacted with them?

- How many different kinds are there?

- How long do they live?

Places to look for answers: library books, field guides, Internet search, encyclopedia, local aquarium.

Grade Three | 397

Day 1

Materials

- *Into the Sea*
- "Ways to Present Nonfiction Information" chart from Week 1
- Collected nonfiction texts from Week 1
- A marker

Exploring Nonfiction

In this lesson, the students:

- Hear, read, and discuss expository nonfiction about animals
- Write about what they learned and what they are curious about
- Share materials fairly

GETTING READY TO WRITE

 ### Briefly Review Nonfiction

Gather the class with partners sitting together, facing you. Remind the students that last week they began exploring nonfiction writing, or writing that gives true information about real things. Explain that they will continue to hear, read, and discuss nonfiction this week in preparation for selecting an animal to research and write about next week.

Direct the students' attention to the "Ways to Present Nonfiction Information" chart and review the listed items. Remind the students that the chart shows different ways that information can be organized and presented in nonfiction.

Show the cover of *Into the Sea* and read the title and the author's and illustrator's names aloud. Tell the students that in this nonfiction book the author gives a lot of information about the life cycle of sea turtles. Explain that you will read parts of the book today. Encourage the students to think about how the author presents this information.

2 Read and Discuss Parts of *Into the Sea*

Read pages 3–10, slowly and clearly, showing the illustrations. Then explain that you will flip to the middle of the book and read just a few sentences from it before reading the last few pages. Show and read the first two sentences on pages 10, 15, 22, and 23. Then read pages 24–29 aloud, showing the illustrations.

> **ELL Vocabulary**
>
> English Language Learners may benefit from discussing the following vocabulary:
>
> **glistens:** shines (p. 5)
> **camouflage:** to blend in as a way to hide (p. 8)

3 Discuss the Story

Ask and briefly discuss:

Q *What did you find out about sea turtles?*

Q *How does the author present the information about sea turtles?*

Point out that the author tells us about the lives of sea turtles by following one turtle through her life cycle: beginning with hatching from an egg, through her maturity to an adult turtle, to eventually laying her own eggs. We learn about what the turtle looks like, how she uses her body, how she finds food, and other details about her.

Explain that this is another way to organize and present information about animals in a nonfiction book. Add *following one individual* to the "Ways to Present Nonfiction Information" chart.

Explain that during writing time, the students will continue to explore animals they are curious about. Encourage them to read today about an animal they have not yet read about. Remind them of your expectations regarding handling of collected materials, and have the students return to their seats.

WRITING TIME

 ### Read Nonfiction Texts

Have the students spend 15–20 minutes browsing the nonfiction materials and reading about animals they are curious about. Interested students might visit the school library or search the Internet. Be ready to assist students in thinking of animals and finding information about them.

 ### Write About What They Read

Call for the students' attention and have them close their books and other materials. Ask and briefly discuss:

Q *When reading today, what did you notice about how the information you looked at is organized?*

Q *What did you find out from your reading today and what are you curious about?* [pause] *Turn to your partner.*

Have the students open their writing notebooks to the next blank page. Write the following tasks on the board and have them work silently for 10–15 minutes.

- Write one or two interesting things you found out about an animal today.

- Write one or two things you are curious about.

- Add any new topics that interest you in the writing ideas section.

As the students write, walk around and observe. Signal to let the students know when writing time is over.

SHARING AND REFLECTING

▶6 Reflect on Writing

Ask and briefly discuss:

Q *So far you've had a chance to hear and read several nonfiction texts. What have you learned about nonfiction?*

Q *What are some different ways that you've noticed nonfiction authors organize and present information?*

As volunteers share ways authors communicate nonfiction, add any methods not yet listed to the "Ways to Present Nonfiction Information" chart.

Invite interested students to read aloud what they wrote in their notebooks today.

Day 2

Materials

- *Little Panda*
- *Into the Sea* from Day 1
- Collected nonfiction texts

Exploring Nonfiction

In this lesson, the students:

- Hear, read, and discuss expository nonfiction about animals
- Write about what they learned and what they are curious about
- Share materials fairly
- Ask one another questions about their writing

GETTING READY TO WRITE

1 ▶ Discuss Curiosity

Gather the class with partners sitting together, facing you. Review that the students have been developing their curiosity about animals and that it is important for nonfiction writers to be curious about many things. Point out that learning a little bit about an animal can often lead to greater curiosity about it. Ask and briefly discuss:

Q *What animals are you curious about now that you weren't as curious about before? What has helped you become curious?*

Encourage the students to continue to develop their curiosity as they explore and read about animal topics that interest them. Explain that you will read from another animal book today, and invite the students to think about what they are curious about as they listen.

2 ▶ Read and Discuss Parts of *Little Panda*

Show the cover of *Little Panda* and read the title and author's name aloud. Explain that the author, Joanne Ryder, is a well-known children's author who has written many books about the animal world. Explain that you will read a few pages of *Little Panda* to show the students another way to present information in nonfiction.

Read pages 3–11 of *Little Panda* slowly and clearly, showing the photographs.

ELL Vocabulary

English Language Learners may benefit from discussing the following vocabulary:

fragile: delicate; easy to break (p. 8)

eager: anxious; wants something very much (p. 11)

Ask and briefly discuss:

Q   *What have you found out so far about pandas?*

Flip through a few more pages of *Little Panda*, showing the photographs. Point out that the author uses the photographs to help her tell the story of the panda. She begins with photos of a newborn panda and continues through his life. She writes words to explain what is happening in the pictures, and the text and the photographs work together. If either of them were taken away, the book would not be complete. Show the cover of *Into the Sea* and briefly discuss:

Q   *How is* Little Panda *similar to* Into the Sea? *How is it different?*

> **Students might say:**
>
> "Both *Little Panda* and *Into the Sea* tell about how one animal grows up."
>
> "*Little Panda* has photographs. *Into the Sea* has illustrations that someone drew."

Explain that during writing time, the students will continue to browse the nonfiction materials and read about animals they are curious about. Encourage them to notice books that give information through photographs. Also encourage them to read about an animal today that they have not yet explored. Remind the students of your expectations regarding handling of collected materials and have them return to their seats.

WRITING TIME

▶ 3 Read Nonfiction Texts

Have the students spend 15–20 minutes browsing the nonfiction materials and reading about animals they are curious about. Interested students might visit the school library or search the Internet. Be ready to assist students in thinking of animals and finding information about them.

Teacher Note ▶

As the students work, ask individuals what they notice about how information is organized in the sources they are reading.

▶ 4 Write About What They Read

Call for the students' attention and have them close their books and other materials. Ask and briefly discuss:

Q *When reading today, what did you notice about how the information you looked at is organized?*

 Q *What did you find out from your reading today and what are you curious about?* [pause] *Turn to your partner.*

Have the students open their writing notebooks to the next blank page. Write the following tasks on the board and have them work silently for 10–15 minutes.

- Write one or two interesting things you found out about an animal today.

- Write one or two things you are curious about.

- Add any new topics that interest you in the writing ideas section.

As the students write, walk around and observe. Signal to let the students know when writing time is over.

SHARING AND REFLECTING

5▶ **Reflect on Writing**

Invite interested students to read aloud what they wrote in their notebooks today. As the students share, discuss as a class:

Q   *What can we ask [Manolo] about what he shared?*

Q   *What did you hear that makes you curious about [Manolo's] animal?*

Day 3

Materials

- *Where Butterflies Grow*
- "Ways to Present Nonfiction Information" chart
- Collected nonfiction texts
- A marker

 Note

You might rephrase this question in the following way:

Q (Show the cover of *Little Panda*.) *Close your eyes and pretend you're a panda. Where are you?*

Q *What do you feel like?*

Q *What are you doing?*

Exploring Nonfiction

In this lesson, the students:

- Hear, read, and discuss expository nonfiction
- Quick-write from an animal's point of view
- Write about what they learned and what they are curious about
- Share materials fairly

GETTING READY TO WRITE

 Briefly Review *Little Panda*

Gather the class with partners sitting together, facing you. Review that the students heard parts of two nonfiction texts this week: *Into the Sea* and *Little Panda*. From those books, they saw that a nonfiction book can follow one animal from birth until adulthood and also use illustrations or photographs to help tell the story.

Direct the students' attention to the "Ways to Present Nonfiction Information" chart and review the items on it. Add *use illustrations or photographs* to the chart.

Ask and briefly discuss:

Q *From hearing parts of* Little Panda, *what do you think it might be like to actually be a panda?*

Students might say:

"I would get used to eating lots of bamboo!"

"It would be interesting to take care of such a tiny baby."

"I would be covered with fur and walk on four legs."

Tell the students that you will read a book today in which the author invites us to imagine being a small animal.

2 ▶ Read *Where Butterflies Grow* Aloud

Show the cover of *Where Butterflies Grow* and read the title and the author's and illustrator's names aloud. Remind the students that Joanne Ryder also wrote *Little Panda*. Read the story aloud, showing the illustrations and stopping as described below.

ELL Vocabulary

English Language Learners may benefit from discussing the following vocabulary:

acrobat: someone who does flips and other tricks (p. 8)

Stop after:

p. 7　　"When the wind tickles your leaf, you and your world shake."

Ask:

Q　*What do you notice about how the author is presenting the information so far? Turn to your partner.*

Without stopping to discuss this question as a class, reread the last sentence and continue reading to the end of the book.

3 ▶ Discuss the Reading

Ask and briefly discuss the following question. Be ready to reread from the book to help the students recall what they heard. Ask:

Q　*How does Joanne Ryder present information about butterflies in this book?*

If necessary, point out that the author writes in a way that allows the reader to imagine what it would be like to be the butterfly. On the "Ways to Present Nonfiction Information" chart, add *imagine life from an animal's point of view*.

Quick-Write: Imagine Being an Animal

Ask the students to close their eyes and think quietly about the following questions. Ask the questions one at a time, pausing between each question to give the students time to think.

Q *If you could be any animal for a day, what would you be?*

Q *Imagine having that animal's body. What does it feel like?*

Q *What do you see from that animal's eyes? What do you hear? Smell?*

Q *You're hungry. What are you looking for to eat? When you've found it, what is it like to eat it?*

Have the students open their eyes, turn to the next blank page in their notebooks, and write for 5 minutes about being the animal they imagined. Tell them to start their writing with the sentence, *I am a _____.*

After about 5 minutes, ask partners to share their writing with each other. After the partners have talked, ask a few volunteers to read their writing to the class.

Explain that during writing time, the students may continue the piece they started during the quick-write or browse the nonfiction materials and read about other animals they are curious about. If they want to continue their quick-write, encourage them to look for more information about the animal they imagined so that what they write is as realistic as possible.

Remind the students of your expectations regarding handling of collected materials, and have them return to their seats.

WRITING TIME

 Read Nonfiction Texts

Have the students spend 15–20 minutes continuing what they started in the quick-write or browsing the nonfiction materials and reading about animals they are curious about. Interested students might visit the school library or search the Internet. Assist students as necessary.

 ## 6 Write About What They Read

Call for the students' attention and have them close their books and other materials. Ask and briefly discuss:

Q *When reading today, what did you notice about how the information you looked at is organized?*

 Q *What did you find out from your reading today and what are you curious about?* [pause] *Turn to your partner.*

Have the students open their writing notebooks to the next blank page. Write the following tasks on the board and have them work silently for 10–15 minutes.

- Write one or two interesting things you found out about an animal today.

- Write one or two things you are curious about.

- Add any new topics that interest you in the writing ideas section.

As the students write, walk around and observe. Signal to let the students know when writing time is over.

SHARING AND REFLECTING

 ## 7 Reflect on Writing

Invite interested students to read aloud what they wrote today in their notebooks. As the students share, discuss as a class:

Q *What can we ask [Justine] about what she shared?*

Q *What did you hear that makes you curious about [Justine's] animal?*

 ELL Note

Next week partners will begin working on a joint nonfiction piece about an animal they agree to research. If you have beginning English speakers, consider having them join an existing pair of fluent English speakers for this project. While you will need to provide support to trios to make sure pairs are integrating the third student and that they are sharing the work fairly, the benefit to ELLs of having two fluent English speakers to interact with and listen to will make this additional support worthwhile.

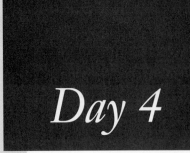

Day 4

Materials

- "About Joanne Ryder" (page 415)
- A sheet of lined paper for each pair
- Collected nonfiction texts
- *Assessment Resource Book*

 Note

If you have decided to have ELL students join existing pairs, give the trios a few minutes to talk informally and get to know each other before they begin to work together.

Meeting an Author and Pair Conferring

In this lesson, the students:

- Learn about a professional author's writing practice
- Identify and list animals they are curious about
- Reach agreement before making decisions
- Make fair decisions

GETTING READY TO WRITE

1 ▶ Read About Joanne Ryder

Gather the class with partners sitting together, facing you. Remind them that this week they heard parts of two nonfiction animal books by Joanne Ryder, *Little Panda* and *Where Butterflies Grow*. Ask and briefly discuss:

Q *Based on hearing these two books, what kind of person do you think Joanne Ryder might be?*

Explain that you will share some information about Joanne Ryder. Ask the students to think as they listen about what Joanne Ryder might be like.

Read "About Joanne Ryder" aloud slowly and clearly. First in pairs and then as a class, discuss:

 Q *What did you learn about Joanne Ryder's interest in animals? Turn to your partner.*

Review Writing from Past Two Weeks

Explain that to get ready to choose an animal to research and write about next week, partners will list the animals they've explored up until now, identify any other animals of interest to them, and narrow down their list.

Have the students spend a few moments quietly rereading the writing in their own notebooks and circling any animal names they see.

 ## Make a Joint List of Animals

Explain that part of the writing process is to have choices of topics to write about. Today partners will develop a joint list of animals they have read and written about so far. Provide each pair with a sheet of lined paper and have partners put their names on it.

Give partners a few minutes to make a joint list of all of the animals they've written about to date.

 ## Identify Other Animals That Interest Them

When most pairs have completed their lists, call for their attention and ask:

Q *What animals did both you and your partner read and write about?*

Q *Which animals on your list do both of you want to know more about? Turn to your partner.*

Explain that today pairs will find at least two more animals that both partners might be interested in researching and writing about. Suggest that they explore animals that live in very different environments from animals they have listed so far (such as insects, creatures that live in the ocean, birds, etc.). Explain that after they have added two more animals to their joint list, they may use the nonfiction resources to learn more about any of the animals on their list. Ask:

Q *What can you and your partner do to be sure you both agree before adding an animal to your list? Why will that be important?*

WRITING TIME

▶5 Identify Other Animals That Interest Them

Give partners ample time to add at least two more animals they are both curious about to their list.

CLASS ASSESSMENT NOTE

Circulate among pairs and observe. Ask yourself:

- Are pairs staying on task, using the resources and discussing the animals of interest to them?

- Are pairs agreeing on animals to add to their list?

- Are they able to find information about the animals they've chosen?

Help struggling pairs by asking them questions such as:

Q *What animals are you thinking about adding to your list?*

Q *If you can't agree on whether or not to add [cheetahs] to your list, what can you do?*

Q *If you can't find information on the animal you're thinking about, what other animal could you consider?*

Record your observations in the *Assessment Resource Book*.

Call for the students' attention and have them put away their books and other materials. Ask and briefly discuss:

Q *How did you make decisions about the animals to add to your list? How was that fair?*

Q *What problems did you have making fair decisions? What might you do differently next time?*

▶6 Narrow the Lists

Explain that partners will review their joint list and circle three animals that they are both interested in researching and writing about. Use "Think, Pair, Share" to have partners first think about and then discuss:

Q *How will you and your partner narrow your list so you are both happy with your choices?* [pause] *Turn to your partner.*

Students might say:

"We can go through the list together and pick three that we both are curious about."

"We can each pick six and see if we have three the same and choose those."

"Maybe I could agree to one animal my partner really likes, he could agree to one I really like, and we could find one we both like."

Give partners a few minutes to agree on and circle three animals. Explain that next week they will decide together on one of the three animals to research and write about.

SHARING AND REFLECTING

 Reflect on Pair Work

Ask and discuss:

Q *Today you and your partner worked together to make the first of many decisions you will make during this unit. Why is it important that you both agree before making a decision?*

Q *Why is it important that your decision feels fair to both of you?*

Q *How are we doing with building a caring writing community in our class? Why do you think so?*

Q *What can we do to continue to make this a safe place for everyone to write and share their thinking?*

Teacher Note

If the students have difficulty answering this question, suggest some ideas such as those in the "Students might say" note. Then ask, "What are some other ways you might choose animals?"

FACILITATION TIP

During this unit, we invite you to focus on **pacing class discussions** so that they are lively and focused without dragging, losing participants, or wandering off the topic. Class discussions should be long enough to allow thinking and short enough to sustain attention. Good pacing requires careful observation of the class (not just the students who are responding) and the timely use of various pacing techniques. To speed up a discussion:

• Call on just a few students to respond to each question, even if others have their hands up.

• Use "Turn to Your Partner" if many students want to speak. Then call on just two or three students to share with the whole class.

To deepen or refocus a discussion:

• Restate the original question if the discussion goes off the topic.

• Ask pairs to discuss whether they agree or disagree with what a classmate has just said.

• Use wait-time before calling on anyone to respond.

EXTENSION

Explore Other Poetic Books By Joanne Ryder

Consider reading other books by Joanne Ryder that use poetic language to give factual information about nonfiction topics, including *The Snail's Spell*, *Shark in the Sea*, and *Earthdance*.

About Joanne Ryder

from *The Big Book of Picture-Book Authors and Illustrators,* by James Preller

As a child growing up in Lake Hiawatha, New Jersey, and Brooklyn, New York, Joanne loved playing outdoors. In Lake Hiawatha, where Joanne lived for her first five years, there were always animals to encounter. Joanne fondly recalls, "It was a wonderful place to explore, full of treasures to discover. There were just a few houses on our street, but there were woods all around, filled with small creatures."

Joanne's parents influenced her deeply…. She warmly remembers, "My father liked to pick things up and examine them. He was the one who introduced me to nature up close. He would hold little creatures in his hand and say, 'Joanne, I have something really fabulous to show you.' Then he would open his fingers and show me whatever it was he had found—a beetle, a snail, a fuzzy caterpillar. Then he would let me hold it, and I could feel it move, wiggle, or crawl as I held it in my hand. So I became very comfortable holding tiny animals."

In many of Joanne's books about nature, she invites readers to let loose their imagination. Combining fantasy and factual insight, they are asked to become another creature—to creep on long padded toes like a lizard, to shake the snow from their fur like a great bear, to stuff acorns inside their furry cheeks like a chipmunk. The journey is always strange and exciting, filled with wonder and delight.

Joanne loves her life as a writer. She tells this story: "When I see kids on school visits, I ask them, 'What do you think I do as a writer?' They say that I sit at a desk and write. I show them a photograph of me walking in Golden Gate Park and say, 'This is me hard at work!' A writer can be working even when he or she is outside looking at a tree. There are so many things around you that can trigger your imagination and fill your mind with images and words."

Week 3 Overview

GENRE: EXPOSITORY NONFICTION

Writing Focus

- Students select an animal to research and write about.

- Students do preresearch writing about their animal.

- Students identify and use various sources of information.

- Students take notes in their own words.

- Students cultivate curiosity.

Social Focus

- Students make decisions and solve problems respectfully.

- Students work in a responsible way.

- Students act in fair and caring ways.

DO AHEAD

- Prior to Day 1, decide on an animal that you will use to model the process of researching and writing an informational piece (for example, dolphins). Collect resources about that animal such as books or information printed from online sources. Think ahead about what you know about the animal you've chosen.

- Prior to Day 2, generate four or five topics about the animal you've chosen to use for modeling (for example, habitat, food, reproduction, and predators). Identify passages in your sources that give information about these topics.

- Prior to Day 2, decide if you will allow small groups of students to visit the library, media center, computer lab, or other locations in the school to research their animals during writing time. Arrange for this ahead of time with the librarian or other adults in the school.

"Get your facts first, then you can distort them as you please."
— *Mark Twain*

Choose another animal from the list you made and repeat the activity you did in Week 2. Write five questions that you have about the animal and see if you can find answers to your questions at the library, on the Internet, or through other sources.

Day 1

Materials

- Read-aloud books from Weeks 1 and 2
- Chart paper and a marker
- *Assessment Resource Book*

Selecting Topics

In this lesson, the students:

- Select an animal to research and write about
- Do pre-research writing about their animal
- Reach agreement before making decisions
- Make fair decisions
- Cultivate curiosity

About Supporting Partner Work

In this unit, partners work together to produce a nonfiction piece about an animal they are both curious about. The content of their writing in this unit will consist primarily of factual information that they have researched in books and other sources. The partner work is intended to support the students by forcing discussion about the facts they are finding, what those facts mean, whether they want to include those facts in their written piece, and how they will write about those facts in their own words.

Both partners are responsible for the form and content of the final product, and each partner is responsible for researching and writing a part. During this process, partners talk about their thinking and learn from each other as they negotiate to reach agreements and make decisions together.

The cooperative work in this unit may challenge your students. The goals are for them to learn how to handle problems when they arise and to make decisions that both partners think are fair. If you notice partners struggling to work together, use these occasions as learning opportunities. Ask questions such as:

Q *What problem are you trying to solve? Why is it important to solve it?*

Q *What is a solution you can both live with, even if it's not your first choice?*

Q *Is that solution fair to both of you? Why or why not?*

GETTING READY TO WRITE

 Briefly Review

Gather the class with partners sitting together, facing you. Have them bring their notebooks and pencils with them. Review that they have been hearing and discussing various kinds of nonfiction about animals and exploring animals of interest to them.

Show the covers and briefly review the read-aloud books the students heard during the past two weeks. Ask and briefly discuss:

Q *As we've read about different animals over the past two weeks, what have you become curious about?*

Explain that in the coming weeks, partners will work together to explore and write a nonfiction informational piece on an animal they are curious about. Like the authors of the books they have heard, they will write to satisfy their own curiosity and to help others learn and become curious about their animal. They will then publish their pieces and put them in the nonfiction section of their class library.

 ## 2 Discuss and Select Topics

Remind the students that last week partners selected three animals that they are both curious about. Have pairs review their three choices.

Signal for their attention and explain that pairs will select one of the three animals on their list to research and write about in the coming weeks. Ask and briefly discuss:

Q *What can you do to make sure you choose an animal that both you and your partner are curious about?*

Have pairs talk about animals and choose one. Encourage them to choose one that they are both very curious about. When most pairs are finished, call for their attention. Ask and briefly discuss:

Q *How did you and your partner make your decision? What's another way a pair decided?*

Q *What problems did you have making the decision? How did you handle those problems?*

Have pairs, one at a time, report the animal they will research to you. If many pairs have chosen the same animal, you might use this opportunity to discuss the need to provide the class library with

 ELL Note

Monitor trios of students to make sure that ELLs are participating in selecting the animal for their trio to research.

information about a greater variety of animals. Ask if any pairs are willing to research a second choice.

▶3 Model Pre-research Writing About an Animal

Tell the students that you've selected an animal that you are curious about. You will research and write nonfiction about this animal to model for the students what they will do in the coming weeks. Name the animal (for example, dolphins; see "Do Ahead" on page 417).

Explain that today the students will do some "pre-research" writing about their animal to find out what they already know, or think they know, about it. Direct their attention to a blank sheet of chart paper and write the name of your animal across the top. Ask them to watch as you think aloud about what you know, or think you know, about this animal, and write several sentences on the chart.

> *Dolphins*
>
> Dolphins live in the sea, but they breathe air. They are mammals, so that means they give birth to baby dolphins, rather than laying eggs. They are smart and friendly. Their diet is mainly small fish.

Explain that each partner will do pre-research writing about the pair's chosen animal in his or her own notebook; then partners will share what they have written with each other. Encourage the students to write freely about everything they know, or think they know, about their animal.

WRITING TIME

 Do Pre-research Writing

Have the students spend 15–20 minutes writing what they know, or
think they know, about their animal. Join the students in writing for
a few minutes; then walk around the room and observe.

CLASS ASSESSMENT NOTE

Observe the students as they write and ask yourself:

- Do the students write freely and with interest about
  their animal?

If you notice students having difficulty writing, ask them to
tell you what they think they know about their animal. You
might also ask whether they've written anything about this
animal in the past two weeks. If so, have them review what
they wrote. If not, ask them to write what they are curious
to know.

Record your observations in the *Assessment Resource Book*.

Signal to let the students know when writing time is over.

SHARING AND REFLECTING

 Reflect in Pairs on Pre-research Writing

Have partners read and discuss their pre-research writing with each
other. After they have had time to share, ask and briefly discuss:

Q *What did your partner write about your animal that you
didn't write?*

Teacher Note

Collect any additional resources you can find related to your students' chosen animals. Save your charted pre-research writing to use on Day 2 and throughout the unit.

Use "Think, Pair, Share" to have partners first think about and then discuss:

 Q *What are some things that you and your partner both wonder about your animal?* [pause] *Turn to your partner.*

After partners have shared, have a few pairs share their thinking with the class. Explain that tomorrow partners will continue to discuss what they are curious about and then begin their research.

Day 2

Selecting Topics

In this lesson, students:

- Review and discuss pre-research writing
- Choose topics to research about their animal
- Identify and use various sources of information
- Cultivate curiosity
- Reach agreement before making decisions
- Make fair decisions

GETTING READY TO WRITE

 Discuss Pre-research Writing

Gather the class with partners sitting together, facing you. Review that partners selected an animal to research and write about together and that they did pre-research writing about it yesterday. Remind them that the purpose of pre-research writing is to help them see what they already know, or think they know, and to determine what they want to find out.

Direct the students' attention to your charted pre-research writing from yesterday, and read it aloud. Think aloud about particular things you want to find out more about, based on what you wrote. Record these as questions on a sheet of chart paper.

Questions About Dolphins

- Are baby dolphins born knowing how to swim?

- How long can a dolphin hold its breath?

- Do dolphins eat anything else besides fish?

- How many years can a dolphin live?

Materials

- Your charted pre-research writing from Day 1
- A sheet of loose, lined paper for each pair
- Collected nonfiction texts from Weeks 1 and 2
- Two sheets of chart paper and a marker

◀ **Teacher Note**

You might say, "I'd like to know if baby dolphins are born knowing how to swim. I also wonder about how long dolphins can hold their breath and if they eat anything besides fish."

Explain that today partners will review their pre-research writing and brainstorm at least five questions about their chosen animal.

 Review Pre-research Writing and Brainstorm Questions

Ask the students to individually reread their pre-research writing from yesterday. Distribute a sheet of lined paper to each pair and ask partners to agree on and write at least five questions about their chosen animal that both partners are curious about.

After partners have had time to generate a few questions, signal for their attention and have several pairs report their questions to the class. As they share, record their questions on a sheet of chart paper entitled "Examples of Research Questions."

Examples of Research Questions

- How long does a baby kangaroo live in its mother's pouch?

- Are zebras born with stripes?

- Do chimps have their own language?

- Does anything eat whales?

- How do polar bears catch fish to eat when everything is frozen solid?

Explain that during writing time today, partners may add to their list of questions and then begin looking for information about their animals using various sources of information.

 Discuss Searching for Resources

Explain that pairs may use multiple sources, including the nonfiction books you've gathered for the class, other books or media materials available in the classroom or school library, or online resources. Ask partners to discuss:

Q *Where might you and your partner go to look for information about your animal?*

If you have decided to have groups of students visit the library, media center, or other locations in the school to look for resources, discuss how the students will take responsibility for themselves outside the classroom. Discuss questions such as:

Q *What will you do to act in a considerate and responsible way at the [library]? Why is that important?*

WRITING TIME

4 ▶ Add to Research Questions and Search for Information

Write the following tasks on the board and have students write silently for 20–30 minutes.

- Add to your list of questions about your animal.

- Search for information about your animal.

Be ready to assist pairs in writing questions and finding information about their animals.

Signal to let the students know when writing time is over.

◀ **Teacher Note**

If your students have access to computers but are not familiar with searching for information online, you might enlist a parent volunteer or an older student to teach small groups of students how to use a search engine. Alternatively, you might do the Extension activity on page 426 to teach the class some strategies for online searches. Encourage the students to print out information they find about their questions.

SHARING AND REFLECTING

5 ▶ Reflect on Taking Responsibility During the Information Search

Ask and briefly discuss:

Q *What did you and your partner do today to act responsibly as you looked for resources?*

Teacher Note

Save your charted research questions about your animal for use on Day 3 and throughout the unit.

Q *What problems did you have? What can you do tomorrow to avoid those problems? Why will it be important for you to try to avoid those problems?*

Explain that pairs will continue to research their animals tomorrow. Have them place their sheet of questions and any other loose papers in their writing folders. If they have identified books or other resources about their topics, they may keep them in their desks to use tomorrow.

EXTENSION

Explore Using Effective Keywords in Internet Searches

If your students are researching their animals on the Internet, consider providing some instruction on how to use effective keywords when doing online searches. Using the animal topic from your model writing in this unit, discuss questions such as:

Q *I want to find out some specific information about how [dolphins raise their young]. When I search the Internet using the keyword ["dolphins"], I get thousands of links that may or may not have the information I want. What word can I add to ["dolphins"] in my search to find information about [how they raise their young]?*

Write the students' suggestions on the board (for example, *dolphin babies, dolphin reproduction, dolphins raising young*).

Have partners talk about what specific information they want to know about their animal and together write a list of keywords they might use to search for that information. Take time after research periods to have pairs share which keywords yielded the information they were looking for and which did not.

Day 3

Researching and Taking Notes

In this lesson, the students:

- Identify and use various sources of information
- Take notes in their own words
- Reach agreement before making decisions
- Share the work fairly

About Teaching Note-taking Skills

In grade 3, the students focus on identifying interesting information about their animal; summarizing the information and writing notes in their own words; and categorizing their notes in preparation for writing. This process lays the foundation for work they continue in grades 4 and 5, in which they focus on narrowing their research topics, writing notes about specific research topics, and identifying source information for their notes.

In this unit, the students take notes on index cards. The cards help them be succinct in writing notes and help them organize their notes in preparation for writing.

Be aware that writing notes in their own words can be challenging for elementary students. Look for opportunities to model this skill frequently, asking the students to help you restate written information in their own words. Monitor and encourage the students but do not worry if you notice them copying from the text, as many of them will not master taking notes until they are older.

GETTING READY TO WRITE

 Briefly Review

Gather the class with partners sitting together, facing you. Review that together partners selected an animal to research and write a nonfiction informational piece about. They wrote about what they think they know about their animal and then brainstormed questions about it.

Explain that today they will begin to research their animal, both to confirm what they think they know and to learn things they are

Materials

- Sources of information about your animal (see "Do Ahead" on page 417)
- Your charted research questions about your animal from Day 2
- Index cards for student note taking and rubber bands
- Collected nonfiction texts
- Chart paper and a marker
- *Assessment Resource Book*

◀ **Teacher Note**

This lesson may require an extended class period.

curious about. Partners will work together to research and take notes about things they want to include in their informational piece.

2 Model Researching and Taking Notes

Ask the students to watch as you model how you would like them to take notes. Use the following procedure to model:

Teacher Note ▶

If possible, model using a table of contents, index, glossary, and/or the Internet to locate information about your animal.

- Reread your charted list of questions and identify one that you found some information about.

- Show the sources of information you found about your animal.

- Read the information in that source aloud.

- Think aloud about the information you read.

- On a sheet of chart paper, model writing a note in your own words. Also model writing your initials in an upper corner of the paper.

Teacher Note ▶

You might say, "I found some information about my question, *Do dolphins eat anything else besides fish?* I did an Internet search with the keywords *dolphins* and *diet* and found a website about dolphins. I printed out some information from that website. It says that dolphins eat nearly one third of their weight in one day. They feed on squid and small schooling fish. This tells me that dolphins eat a whole lot every day. It would be like me eating 50 pounds of fish and squid every day!"

> *CW*
>
> They eat squid and small fish. They eat about one third of their body weight each day. That would be like me eating 50 pounds of food every day!

Point out that in finding information about your question, you found other interesting information to include in your piece.

Use this procedure to model another example of taking notes. Point out that notes are most helpful when they are brief and written in the writer's own words, rather than copied exactly from the source.

Explain that the students will take their notes on index cards, one note per card. Point out that having the notes on cards will help the students organize them when they get ready to write their informational piece. Remind them to write both partners' initials on each card.

 Get Ready to Work Together

Have partners reread their list of brainstormed questions from yesterday. Explain that the questions are just starting places; they should look for and take notes about any information that they find interesting about their animal.

Explain that partners will need to work together to research and take notes about their animal. Ask and briefly discuss:

Q *What will you and your partner do to share your work fairly today?*

Q *What can you and your partner do if you don't agree at first about whether to take notes about a piece of information?*

> **Students might say:**
>
> "We'll read a book together and stop when we want to write a note about something."
>
> "We'll each look in a different book but talk to each other about interesting things we read so we can take notes about them."
>
> "We can take turns writing the notes."
>
> "If we don't agree, we can tell our partner why we think something is interesting enough to take notes on."

Encourage partners to try the things they suggested, and tell them that you will check in with them to see how they did.

◀ **Teacher Note**

If partners have difficulty suggesting ways to share the work, offer some ideas like those in the "Students might say" note. Then ask, "What else can you do to share the work?"

WRITING TIME

 Research Animal Topics and Take Notes

Distribute the cards to the students and have them begin researching and taking notes about their animals. During this time, they may talk in soft voices about their work.

◀ **Teacher Note**

Some pairs may still be looking for resources today. This is to be expected. On any given day, you are likely to have pairs working at different stages of their projects.

As the students write, circulate and observe.

CLASS ASSESSMENT NOTE

Observe the students and ask yourself:

* Are partners agreeing on interesting facts to write about their animal?

* Are they writing notes in their own words?

* Are they writing just one note per card?

* Are they sharing the work?

If necessary, stop the class to remind the students of the procedures to follow when taking their notes. If you notice partners having difficulty sharing the work, stop them and discuss questions such as:

Q *What are each of you responsible for accomplishing during this writing time?*

Q *Is the way you are sharing the work fair? Why or why not?*

Q *What can you do to make it so you are sharing the work fairly?*

Q *Why is it important that both of you do your part of the work on this project?*

Record your observations in the *Assessment Resource Book*.

Signal to let the students know when writing time is over. Remind them to write their initials on all of their cards.

SHARING AND REFLECTING

5 ▶ **Reflect on What the Students Learned**

Have partners review their notes together. Then, as a class, discuss:

Q *What is one interesting fact you and your partner learned about your animal today?*

Q *As you listened to [Donna and Juan] share about their animal topic, what did you hear that makes you curious?*

Q *What was [interesting/challenging] about doing research today? What suggestions do you have that might help someone else with this challenge?*

Point out that curiosity leads to learning, and that learning often leads to more curiosity.

 Reflect on Sharing Work Fairly

Ask and briefly discuss:

Q *How did you and your partner share the work fairly today?*

Q *If you didn't share the work fairly, what will you do tomorrow to share the work fairly? Why will that be important to do?*

Explain that the students will continue to share work fairly as they research their animal tomorrow. Provide the students with rubber bands to bind their cards. Have them put their cards in their writing folders or another secure place until tomorrow.

EXTENSION

Continue Research During Other Times of the Day

You might have the students continue doing research and taking notes during other times of the day. They might use independent time, their library period, or after-school activity time. Also encourage the students to use their public library or home computers to continue their research and writing.

FACILITATION TIP

Continue to focus on **pacing class discussions** so they are neither too short nor too long. Scan the whole class (not just the students who are responding) and use techniques such as the following:

- Call on just a few students to respond to each question, even if others have their hands up.

- Use "Turn to Your Partner" if many students want to speak, then call on just two or three students to share with the whole class.

- Restate the original question if the discussion goes off the topic.

- Ask pairs to discuss whether they agree or disagree with what a classmate has just said.

- Use wait-time before calling on anyone to respond.

Teacher Note

Save your charted research notes to use on Day 4.

Day 4

Materials

- Collected nonfiction texts
- Sources of information about your animal
- Your research notes from Day 3
- Your charted pre-research writing and research questions about your animal
- Index cards and rubber bands
- Chart paper and a marker
- "Conference Notes" record sheet for each pair (BLM1)

Researching and Taking Notes

In this lesson, the students:

- Identify and use various sources of information
- Take notes in their own words
- Reach agreement before making decisions
- Share the work fairly

GETTING READY TO WRITE

1 ▶ Discuss Research Process

Gather the class with partners sitting together, facing you. Review that partners began researching their chosen animal yesterday. Explain that today they will continue to research and take notes about their animal.

Ask partners to reread their list of brainstormed questions as well as their notes from yesterday. Ask and briefly discuss:

Q *What information did you and your partner find that answers any of your questions? Tell us about that.*

Q *What other interesting information have you found about your animal? Tell us about it.*

Teacher Note

You might say, "It says in my source, 'Some dolphins have been seen working together to herd fish into tight balls.' How can I capture that briefly in my own words?" If possible, use the students' suggestions to write a note, such as *Dolphins sometimes work as a team to herd fish together.*

2 ▶ Model Researching and Taking Notes

Ask the students to watch as you model another example of researching and taking notes. Follow the procedure you used yesterday to model locating information, reading it aloud, thinking aloud about it, and writing a note about it in your own words. This time, invite the students to help you write the note.

Model another example using the same procedure.

Explain that the students will continue to research their animals today. Encourage them to take notes about any interesting information they find about their animal, including information about their questions. Remind them to try to write their notes in their own words.

WRITING TIME

 ## Research Animal Topics and Take Notes

Distribute more cards as needed and have the students research and take notes about their topics. As they work, circulate, observe, and offer assistance. When the pairs seem to be working independently, begin conferring with one pair at a time.

TEACHER CONFERENCE NOTE

Today you will begin conferring with pairs and continue conferring with them into the next week. Ask partners to tell you the animal they are each researching and what they are learning about that animal. Focus your conversations on what the partners are curious about, what they are learning, and how they are capturing what they are learning in their notes. Ask questions such as:

Q   *What animal are the two of you researching?*

Q   *What have you found out about that animal? Read me one of your notes.*

Q   *What else do you want to know? Where will you go to try to find out about that?*

If you ask a student to read you a note and you find the note confusing, ask the student what the note means. Explain why you were confused and ask the pair how the note might be rewritten to be more clear.

Document your observations for each pair using the "Conference Notes" record sheet (BLM1). Use the "Conference Notes" record sheets during conferences throughout this unit.

Signal to let the students know when writing time is over. Remind partners to write their initials on each of their cards.

SHARING AND REFLECTING

 Reflect on Research and Taking Notes

Have partners review their notes together to make sure what they have written makes sense. Explain that if they find a note confusing, they should work together to decide what is confusing about it and how to make it more understandable. Explain that partners may need to refer to the source of the note to help them rewrite it.

After several minutes, briefly discuss:

Q *Who has an example of a confusing note? What did you do to make the note more understandable?*

Q *What have you learned about taking notes? What suggestions do you have to help others?*

Q *What did you and your partner do to share the work fairly today?*

Explain that partners will continue to research their animals next week. Have them bind their index cards with a rubber band and place them in their writing folders or another secure place until then.

Teacher Note

Save your charted research notes to use in Week 4.

Week 4 Overview

GENRE: EXPOSITORY NONFICTION

Writing Focus

- Students use various sources of information to research an animal.

- Students take notes in their own words.

- Students organize their notes in preparation for writing.

- Students draft nonfiction informational pieces.

- Students confer with one another and the teacher.

Social Focus

- Students make decisions and solve problems respectfully.

- Students act in fair and caring ways.

- Students work in a responsible way.

DO AHEAD

- Prior to Day 2, look for more information about any unanswered questions on your charted questions about your animal. Take notes so you have eight to ten notes altogether. Think about how you will sort your notes under the headings *habitat*, *physical characteristics*, *reproduction*, *food*, and *other*. (See Day 2, Step 2, on pages 439–442.)

- Prior to Day 3, review your grouped notes (from Day 2) and think ahead about how you might begin drafting an informational piece. Include appropriate information from your pre-research writing as well as from your notes. (See Day 3, Step 2, on pages 446–447.)

- Prior to Day 4, review the informational piece you modeled writing on Day 3 and think ahead about how you will model adding to the piece. (See Day 4, Step 1, on pages 451–452.)

TEACHER AS WRITER

"We write about what we don't know about what we know."
— *Grace Paley*

Reread the questions you wrote about an animal in "Teacher as Writer" during the past two weeks. Choose two questions to research and write about. Ask yourself:

- Is it hard or easy to locate information about my questions? If it's hard, what makes it hard? Would modifying my questions make it easier? How?

- What tools am I using to locate the information (for example, tables of contents, indexes, glossaries, search engines)?

Day 1

Materials

- Collected nonfiction texts
- Sources of information about your animal from Week 3
- Your research notes from Week 3
- Your charted pre-research writing and research questions
- Index cards and rubber bands

Researching and Taking Notes

In this lesson, the students:

- Continue to research animals
- Take notes in their own words
- Check each other's notes for understanding
- Share the work fairly

GETTING READY TO WRITE

1 ▶ Review Pre-research Writing and Notes

Gather the class with partners sitting together, facing you. Remind them to bring their pre-research writing, questions about their animal, and their notes. Review that partners began researching an animal last week. Ask them to quietly reread their pre-research writing and their notes. Signal for their attention and ask:

Q *What are some interesting things you found out about your animal?*

Q *Look at your list of questions. Which has your research helped you answer? Turn to your partner.*

Q *What would you like to find information about today? Turn to your partner.*

2 ▶ Discuss How Partners Will Work Together

Explain that today partners will continue to research and take notes about their animal. Later this week they will begin drafting a nonfiction piece about their animal that will become part of their classroom library. Encourage them to take notes about any interesting information they find about their animal, including information about their questions. Remind them to try to write their notes in their own words.

Teacher Note

If necessary, model researching and taking notes about your animal again, using the procedure you used in Week 3, Day 4, Step 2. Model locating specific information using table of contents, index, glossary, etc. Read information from your source aloud and ask the students to help you write notes that are brief and written in your own words.

Ask partners to spend a few minutes discussing what they want to accomplish today and how they will share the work in a fair way. When they are ready to begin working, have them return to their seats.

WRITING TIME

 ### Continue to Research Animal Topics and Take Notes

Distribute more index cards as needed and have the students research and take notes about their animals. As they work, circulate, observe, and offer assistance. When the pair seem to be working independently, confer with one pair at a time.

TEACHER CONFERENCE NOTE

As you did in Week 3, confer with pairs about their research and about taking notes. Focus your conversations on what the partners are curious about, what they are learning, and how they are capturing what they are learning in their notes. Ask questions such as:

Q *What interesting things have you learned about your animal? Read me your note about that.*

Q *What else do you want to know about your animal? Where will you look for that information?*

Q *Have you found answers to any of your questions? Tell me about them.*

Q *What are you reading now? What is an interesting piece of information that this source tells you? What note could you write?*

Q *How are your sharing the work fairly?*

Document your observations for each pair using the "Conference Notes" record sheet (BLM1).

Signal to let the students know when writing time is over.

SHARING AND REFLECTING

4 ▶ Reflect on Research and Taking Notes

Have partners review their notes together. Ask:

Q   *What was it like to take notes in your own words today? Read us one of your notes.*

Q   *What is one interesting fact that you and your partner learned about your animal today?*

Q   *Take a look at your pre-research writing. What have you learned about your animal that confirms what you thought you knew? What have you learned that's different from what you thought you knew?*

Explain that partners will begin organizing their notes tomorrow in preparation for writing their informational piece. They will have time to continue researching their topic as well.

Provide rubber bands as needed and have partners bind their cards and put them in their writing folders or another secure place until tomorrow.

Teacher Note ▶

If necessary, restate the first part of this question to say, "What have you learned that tells you that what you thought about your animal was correct?"

Day 2

Organizing Notes

In this lesson, the students:

- Organize their notes in preparation for writing
- Reach agreement before making decisions
- Agree and disagree in a caring way
- Share the work fairly

GETTING READY TO WRITE

1 ▶ Briefly Review

Gather the class in a circle with partners sitting together. Review that they have been researching and taking notes about their animals. Explain that in order to write about what they have learned in a clear and interesting way, they will need to organize their notes so they are complete and make sense. Explain that today you will show them how to organize notes. They will then organize their own notes to see where they need more information and to get ready to write.

2 ▶ Model Organizing Notes

Ask the students to watch as you model organizing your notes by topic. Read your notes aloud as you spread them out on the floor. Explain that some of the notes can be put together because they are about the same topic. Model putting similar notes together and naming the categories (see the Teacher Note).

Ask:

Q *What other notes can we put together?*

◀ **Teacher Note**

You might say, "I will put *Instead of gills, they have lungs and breathe air* and *They have teeth and are warm-blooded* together because they both tell about dolphins' physical characteristics. I will call this group of notes 'Physical Characteristics.'"

Continue to model categorizing the notes, grouping them under *Physical Characteristics*, *Habitat*, *Food*, *Reproduction*, and *Other*. Use self-stick notes to label each group.

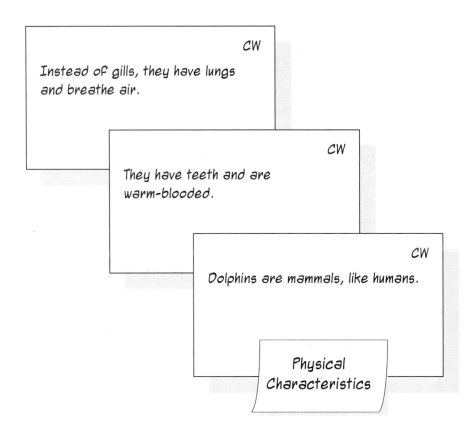

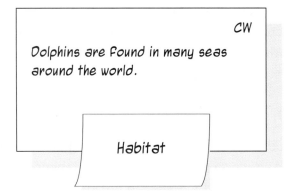

CW

Dolphins sometimes work as a team to herd fish together.

CW

They eat squid and small fish. They eat about one third of their body weight each day. That would be like me eating 50 pounds of food every day!

Food

CW

Dolphins give birth to live young and nurse them.

CW

Baby dolphins are called calves. Calves can breathe and swim alone minutes after being born.

CW

They stay with their mother for one or two years.

Reproduction

FACILITATION TIP

Continue to focus on **pacing class discussions** by scanning the class and using techniques such as the following:

- Call on just a few students to respond to each question.

- Use "Turn to Your Partner" if many students want to speak. Then call on just two or three students to share with the whole class.

- Restate the original question if the discussion goes off the topic.

- Ask pairs to discuss whether they agree or disagree with what a classmate has just said.

- Use wait-time before calling on anyone to respond.

Teacher Note ▶

Prior to Day 3, use the students' suggestions to research and write additional notes so you have several notes in each group.

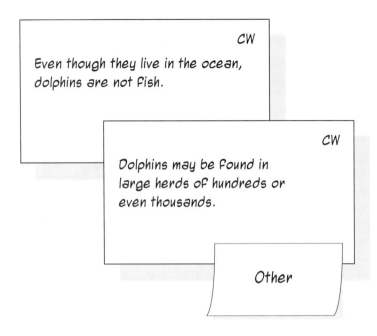

After categorizing all of the notes, point out that these are facts that you will include in your written piece about your topic. Ask:

Q　*Do you think I have enough information for my written piece? Why or why not?*

Q　*Which category do you think might need more information? Why?*

Students might say:

"You only have one note under 'Habitat.' You might want to add a few more to that category."

"Maybe you can include more information about their physical characteristics."

Use paper clips to clip each group of notes together with its heading.

▶ **3　Discuss How Partners Will Work Together**

Explain and write the following tasks on the board:

- Organize your notes into the following groups: Physical Characteristics, Habitat, Food, Reproduction, and Other.

- Label the groups using self-stick notes.

- Decide where you need more information and do more research.

- Clip the groups of notes together with their headings.

Ask and briefly discuss:

Q *If you and your partner disagree at first about how to organize your notes, what will you do?*

Q *Why is it important to disagree in a caring way?*

Point out that disagreements are natural in any learning situation and that people can disagree while maintaining respect for one another. Encourage partners to be aware of how they are disagreeing with each other and tell them that you will check in with them at the end of the lesson.

Have partners spend a few minutes discussing what they will do and how they will share the work in a fair way. When they are ready, have them return to their seats and begin working.

WRITING TIME

 Organize Notes for Writing

Have partners work together for 20–30 minutes to categorize their notes and continue researching their animals. When pairs have finished categorizing their notes, have them signal you so you can review their work.

CLASS ASSESSMENT NOTE

Observe partners working and ask yourself:

- Do partners seem able to categorize their notes in ways that make sense?

- Do they categorize all their notes?

- Are they able to agree on how to categorize their notes?

- If they don't agree at first, do they keep talking until they reach agreement?

continues

Grade Three | 443

CLASS ASSESSMENT NOTE *continued*

Support struggling pairs by asking them questions such as:

Q *What notes seem to belong together? Why do you think so?*

Q *What other notes could go into your "Food" group? Why do you think so?*

Be aware that categorizing information can be challenging for young students; some of their difficulty may be normal for their developmental level. They may have difficulty defining categories or consistently sorting all their notes into those categories. They may want to discard notes that don't fit, or they may become preoccupied with having the same number of notes in each category. Encourage them to try their best to organize all their notes in a way that makes sense.

Record your observations in the *Assessment Resource Book*.

Signal to let the students know when writing time is over.

SHARING AND REFLECTING

 Reflect on Partner Work

Ask:

Q *In which categories did you and your partner decide you needed more information? What made you decide that?*

Q *Did you and your partner disagree about anything when you were organizing your notes? If so, what? What did you do to disagree in a caring way? How did you reach agreement?*

Explain that tomorrow partners will finish organizing their notes, if necessary, and begin writing their informational pieces. Pairs who still need time to finish their research and to take more notes will have time to do so.

Have partners put their work away in a secure place until tomorrow.

Teacher Note

Decide if your students need another day or two to organize their notes and finish their research before moving into the drafting phase. If so, plan time for them to do this work before moving on to Day 3.

EXTENSION

Discuss Elements of Nonfiction Across the School Day

Take time at the end of independent reading periods and other times during the day to discuss the nonfiction that the students are reading. Have students share the title and author's name of the book they are reading and explain what the book is about. Discuss questions such as:

Q *How do you know that the book you are reading is nonfiction?*

Q *What true information are you learning from the book?*

Q *What features (such as illustrations, captions, diagrams, graphs, tables of contents, and glossaries) of nonfiction do you see in your book?*

Day 3

Materials

- Your grouped research notes (see "Do Ahead" on page 435)

- Loose, lined paper for writing drafts

- A folder for each pair

- Chart paper and a marker

- *Assessment Resource Book*

Drafting and Pair Conferring

In this lesson, the students:

- Order their grouped notes to prepare to write

- Decide how they will share the writing fairly

- Begin drafting their informational piece

- Check for understanding

- Reach agreement before making decisions

- Share the work fairly

GETTING READY TO WRITE

1▶ Briefly Review

Gather the class in a circle with partners sitting together. Review that they have grouped their research notes into topics in preparation for writing. Explain that today partners will put their grouped notes in the order in which they want to write about them and that they will then begin writing a draft of their piece. Ask and briefly discuss:

 Q *What have you found out about your animal that you think other people will be curious to learn about? Turn to your partner.*

After partners have talked, signal for their attention and explain that you will model ordering your grouped notes and beginning to write a draft.

Teacher Note

 You might say, "To get my readers' attention from the beginning, I think I'll first write about the physical characteristics that dolphins and humans have in common. Then I will write about where they live and what they eat."

2▶ Model Ordering Your Notes and Beginning a Draft

Ask the students to watch as you spread your clipped groups of notes out on the floor. Think aloud about the order in which you want to write about each category and then stack the groups in that order.

Unclip your first group of notes and spread the notes out on the floor. Reread them and think aloud about how you might want to start writing this section of your piece. Model writing a few sentences about this topic, double-spaced, on a sheet of blank chart paper. Point out the notes you are using as you write. Ask:

Q   *What is another sentence I can write [showing how dolphins are like people]?*

Q   *What shall I tell about next? What sentence can I write to tell about that?*

◀ Teacher Note

You might say, "Maybe I can start by writing, *Dolphins are mammals, just like you and me.*"

Physical Characteristics

Dolphins are mammals, just like you and me. Even though

dolphins live in the sea, they breathe air. While fish have gills

to help them breathe underwater, dolphins have lungs like

humans do.

Use the students' suggestions to write a few more sentences. If the students have difficulty suggesting sentences, model writing a few more yourself. Point out that you are trying to write in a way that makes the topic as interesting as possible for your readers.

▶3 Discuss How Partners Will Work Together

Explain that partners will work together today to order their notes and begin writing. Tell them that you expect both partners to participate in the writing, so they will need to decide who will write what part. They will put their parts together into one piece when they publish it for the class.

ELL Note

Monitor trios of students to make sure that ELLs are participating in the work. Very limited English speakers may not be able to help with the writing. If necessary, help them contribute to their trio's work in other ways, such as reading the research notes aloud, and drawing and labeling diagrams to accompany the final piece.

Explain and write the following tasks on the board:

● Arrange your grouped notes in the order in which you will write about them.

● Reread your notes and make sure the order makes sense.

● Decide how you will share the writing fairly.

● Begin writing a draft of your informational piece, double-spaced, on loose, lined paper.

Ask partners to spend a few minutes discussing what they want to accomplish today and how they will share the work in a fair way. After a moment, signal for attention. Ask and briefly discuss:

Q *What part of your pair work are you responsible for today?*

Have partners return to their seats and begin working.

WRITING TIME

▶ **Begin Drafting Informational Pieces**

Have partners work together for 20–30 minutes to order their notes and draft their informational piece. As the students work, circulate and observe.

CLASS ASSESSMENT NOTE

Observe partners working and ask yourself:

● Do partners seem able to decide on an order of topics for their piece?

● Does the order make sense?

● Are both partners writing sections of their draft?

● Are they able to use their notes to write coherently about their topic?

● Are they double-spacing their drafts?

continues

CLASS ASSESSMENT NOTE *continued*

Support struggling pairs by asking them questions such as:

Q *What do you want to write about first to get your reader's attention?*

Q *What do you want to write about next?*

Q *What part is each partner working on? Is that a fair way to share the work? Why or why not? [What will you do differently to share the work fairly?]*

Record your observations in the *Assessment Record Book*.

Signal to let the students know when writing time is over.

SHARING AND REFLECTING

▶5 Confer in Pairs About Drafts

Have partners read their writing from today to each other and check to make sure they each understand what the other has written. After a few moments, signal for their attention and ask:

Q *Do you understand everything your partner wrote today? If not, what can you ask your partner to help you understand?*

Q *If your partner is confused about something you wrote, how can you revise it to make it clearer?*

Invite volunteers to share examples from their own writing as they answer these questions.

▶6 Reflect on Partner Work

Ask and briefly discuss:

Q *What did you do to work responsibly on your own part of the work today? How did that help your pair work?*

Teacher Note

Save the model draft of your informational piece to use on Day 4.

Q *What did you and your partner do to reach agreement about how to write your informational piece? If you didn't agree at first, what did you do to reach agreement?*

Distribute a folder to each pair and have partners write their names on it. Explain that pairs will keep all of their papers related to their informational pieces in this joint folder. Have the students decide who will keep the folder until tomorrow.

Day 4

Drafting and Pair Conferring

In this lesson, the students:

- Draft their informational piece
- Check for understanding
- Work responsibly in pairs
- Share the work fairly

GETTING READY TO WRITE

1 **Model Adding to Your Draft**

Gather the class in a circle with partners sitting together. Review that they began writing drafts of their informational pieces yesterday. Explain that they will continue to work on their drafts today.

Using the procedure from yesterday (see Day 3, Step 2, on pages 446–447), model adding to your informational piece by spreading a group of notes out on the floor, rereading them, thinking aloud about what you might write, and writing.

Elicit the students' help in coming up with more sentences. Ask questions such as:

Q (Point to a note.) *I want to include this information about [how dolphin calves stay with their mothers for one or two years]. What sentence could I write to get this information across in an interesting way?*

If the students have difficulty suggesting sentences, continue thinking aloud and writing a few more yourself. Point out that you are trying to write in a way that makes the topic as interesting as possible for your readers.

Materials

- Your grouped research notes from Day 3
- Model draft of your informational piece from Day 3
- Loose, lined paper for writing drafts
- Chart paper and a marker

Baby Dolphins

Dolphins give birth to live young and nurse them. Baby dolphins are called calves. Calves can breathe and swim alone right after being born. They stay with their mothers one or two years. Can you imagine only staying with your mother for one or two years?

Encourage the students to continue to think about how to make their topic interesting to their readers as they write today.

▶2 Discuss How Partners Will Work Together

Remind the students that you expect both partners to participate in the writing. They will each write different sections, and then they will put their sections together into one piece when they publish it for the class.

Ask partners to spend a few minutes reviewing what they have written so far and deciding what they will write today. When they are ready, have them return to their seats and begin working.

WRITING TIME

▶3 Draft Informational Pieces

Have partners work together for 20–30 minutes to draft their informational pieces. As they work, circulate, observe, and offer assistance. When pairs seem to be working independently, confer with one pair at a time.

TEACHER CONFERENCE NOTE

Continue to confer with pairs about their drafts. Have partners read their drafts to you. Ask questions such as:

Q *What interesting things you have learned about your animal? Read me your note about that.*

Q *What else do you want to know about your animal? Where will you look for that information?*

Q *Have you found answers to any of your questions? Tell me about them.*

Q *What are you reading now? What is an interesting piece of information that this source tells you? What note could you write?*

Q *How are your sharing the work fairly?*

Document your observations for each pair using the "Conference Notes" record sheet (BLM1).

Signal to let the students know when writing time is over.

SHARING AND REFLECTING

▶4 Confer in Pairs About Drafts

As they did yesterday, have partners read their writing from today to each other and check to make sure they each understand what the other has written. After a few moments, signal for their attention and ask:

Q *Do you understand everything you partner wrote today? If not, what can you ask your partner to help you understand?*

Q *If your partner is confused about something you wrote, how can you revise it to make it clearer?*

Invite volunteers to share examples from their own writing as they answer these questions.

Teacher Note

Save your grouped research notes and your model draft to use in Week 5.

5 ▶ **Reflect on Partner Work**

Ask and briefly discuss:

Q *What did you do to work responsibly on your own part of the work today? How did that help your pair work?*

Q *Did you and your partner disagree about anything today? If so, what did you do to reach agreement?*

Explain that partners will continue to work on their drafts next week.

Week 5 Overview

GENRE: EXPOSITORY NONFICTION

Writing Focus

• Students finish drafting their informational pieces.

• Students explore and integrate expository text features into their pieces.

• Students explore strong opening sentences.

• Students revise their writing with input from others.

• Students confer with one another and the teacher.

Social Focus

• Students make decisions and solve problems respectfully.

• Students act in fair and caring ways.

• Students help one another improve their writing.

• Students work in a responsible way.

• Students build on one another's thinking.

DO AHEAD

• Prior to Day 1, think about where you might add two or three illustrations in your model informational piece and what the accompanying captions might say.

• Prior to Day 3, finish writing your model informational piece.

• Prior to Day 4, decide how you will combine pairs to form groups of four.

Day 1

Materials

- *Reptiles* from Week 1
- Your draft informational piece from Week 4
- Loose, lined paper for writing drafts
- A pad of small 1½" x 2" self-stick notes for each pair

Drafting and Pair Conferring

In this lesson, the students:

- Draft their informational piece
- Explore expository text features
- Decide on illustrations and captions for their piece
- Agree and disagree in a caring way
- Assess how a solution is working and modify it if necessary
- Share the work fairly

GETTING READY TO WRITE

 Reread and Share Sentences

Gather the class with partners sitting together, facing you. Remind the students that last week they began drafting their nonfiction informational pieces. Review that the purpose of these pieces is to help their classmates become curious and learn about their animals by presenting information in an interesting way.

Ask the students to quietly reread their own writing from last week and to select one sentence that they feel might help others become curious about their animal. Tell them that you would like each student to read his sentence aloud. Ask the students to listen carefully to one another's sentences and to think about which ones make them curious.

Go around the room and have the students read their sentences aloud, without comment. When all have read, ask and briefly discuss:

Q *What sentences did you hear that made you curious?*

Explain that the students will continue to work on their drafts today, and encourage them to write in a way that helps others become as curious as they are about their topic.

Discuss Captions and Illustrations

Explain that nonfiction authors often include photographs or illustrations in their texts to provide information and spark interest. Show *Reptiles* and remind the students that they heard this book earlier in the unit. Flip through the book, stopping several times to read a page, show a photograph, and read its caption. For each photograph, ask and briefly discuss:

Q *Why do you think the author included this photograph?*

Q *How does the caption help us understand the photograph?*

> **Students might say:**
>
> "The photograph shows something the author wrote about and helps you understand it."
>
> "She included this picture because it is very [exciting/scary/pretty]."
>
> "The caption explains the picture."
>
> "This caption helps you see something in the picture you might not have seen."

 Model Marking Your Draft for Illustrations and Captions

Explain that partners will decide where in their piece they would like to put some illustrations and captions. Illustrations may be ones the students draw themselves or copies of photographs from magazines or the Internet. Explain that they will place a self-stick note in their draft to show where an illustration might go. The note will remind them to leave space for the illustration and caption when they copy their draft into its final version.

Direct the students' attention to your charted informational piece and explain that you've thought about where it might be helpful to have illustrations and captions in your piece. Point to each place where you might include an illustration in your final draft, and explain why you think it will be helpful to have an illustration there. Write a draft of the caption that will accompany your illustration on a self-stick note and place it where the illustration will go.

FACILITATION TIP

As you continue to focus on **pacing class discussions** this week, ask yourself:

- Do most students stay engaged for the duration of most discussions?

- What do the students look like when they are engaged? What do they look like when they become disengaged?

- What contributes to loss of focus on the part of the students?

- Are the students getting used to me not calling on every student with a hand up?

Continue to practice the techniques listed in the previous Facilitation Tip for speeding up or deepening a discussion.

◀ **Teacher Note**

Remind the students to write a caption for each illustration on a self-stick note and to place it on their draft where the illustration will go.

Discuss How Partners Will Work Together

Explain and write the following tasks on the board:

- Decide where you want to include illustrations and what kind they will be.

- Write captions on self-stick notes and place them in your draft where the illustrations will go.

- Continue drafting your informational piece.

Briefly discuss:

Q *Today you and your partner have many decisions to make. What have you learned about making decisions with a partner that will help you?*

Q *What are some ways to make a fair decision if you and your partner don't agree at first?*

Ask partners to spend a few minutes deciding what they want to accomplish today and how they will share the work fairly. Remind them that both partners need to be writing sections of their joint draft. When they are ready, have them return to their seats.

WRITING TIME

5 **Draft Informational Pieces**

Have partners work on their informational pieces. As they work, circulate, observe, and offer assistance. When pairs seem to be working independently, confer with one pair at a time.

TEACHER CONFERENCE NOTE

As you did in Week 4, continue to confer with pairs about their informational piece. Ask partners to read their drafts aloud and to tell you their plan for their piece. Ask questions such as:

Q *What interesting things have you learned about your animal? Read me your note about that.*

Q *What else do you want to know about your animal? Where will you look for that information?*

Q *Have you found answers to any of your questions? Tell me about them.*

Q *What are you reading now? What is an interesting piece of information that this source tells you? What note could you write?*

Q *How are your sharing the work fairly?*

Document your observations for each pair using the "Conference Notes" record sheet (BLM1).

Signal to let the students know when writing time is over.

SHARING AND REFLECTING

▶ 6 Confer in Pairs and Reflect

As they did in Week 4, have partners read their writing from today to each other and check to make sure they each understand what the other has written. Give them time to clarify any confusion in their writing; then ask and briefly discuss:

Q *What illustrations have you and your partner decided to include? How did you decide?*

Q *If you had difficulty agreeing on illustrations to include, what did you do to try to reach agreement? How did that work?*

Q *What might you want to do differently tomorrow to reach agreement?*

Explain that partners will continue to work on their pieces tomorrow.

Day 2

Materials

- *Student Writing Handbook* page 12
- Your draft informational piece
- Loose, lined paper for writing drafts
- Chart paper and a marker

Analyzing and Revising Drafts

In this lesson, the students:

- Reread their writing critically
- Explore strong opening sentences
- Quick-write opening sentences that capture attention
- Get ideas by listening to others

GETTING READY TO WRITE

 Briefly Review

Have partners sit together at desks today. Review that they are working on drafts of their nonfiction informational pieces, which they will publish for the class library. Remind them that yesterday they discussed including illustrations and captions in their pieces.

Explain that in the next few days, you will help the students think about ways they can add to, revise, and improve their pieces so they are as clear and interesting as possible for their readers.

Point out that in a nonfiction piece, like in all literature, a strong opening helps to get the reader's attention. Explain that the students will spend some time today looking at strong openings for nonfiction and work on the opening sentences of their pieces.

 Discuss Strong Opening Sentences

Ask the students to open to *Student Writing Handbook* page 12, where the opening sentences from three books they heard earlier in the unit are reproduced. Ask them to follow along as you read the first passage aloud. Invite them to think about what the authors are doing in these openings to get readers interested in reading on.

Read the first passage aloud twice:

> "A snake flicks its long tongue as it slithers along the ground.
> A turtle sits on a rotting log and basks in the sun. A crocodile
> grabs a fish with its mighty jaws. These are the images that
> come to mind when someone says the word 'reptile.'"
> (from *Reptiles*)

Ask:

 Q *What do you think the author is doing in this opening to get us interested in reading the book? Turn to your partner.*

Signal for attention and have a few volunteers share their thinking with the class.

> **Students might say:**
>
> "The author describes the animals so that I can see them in
> my mind."
>
> "The author uses interesting words like *slithers* and *flicks* to
> get us interested."

Repeat this procedure with the next two passages:

> "Tap, tap. Scritch. The tiny sea turtle is the last hatchling to break
> out of her leathery egg and crawl up the sides of a sandy nest.
> She is not much bigger than a bottle cap and would make a
> good meal for a hungry sea bird or a crab." (from *Into the Sea*)
>
> "This is a growing place green and warm and bright. Lift up a leaf
> and you may find someone ready to be born. Lift up a leaf and
> imagine…." (from *Where Butterflies Grow*)

Point out that all three authors introduce their topics using opening sentences that are descriptive and that help the reader imagine something interesting about their topic.

▶ 3 Model Writing Strong Openings

Direct the students' attention to your model informational piece. Reread the piece aloud and then think aloud about possible opening sentences for your piece. Write one or two possible openings on a sheet of chart paper and then ask:

Q *What other opening sentences could I write to introduce my topic and to capture my readers' attention?*

Teacher Note

You might say, "I could start my piece with a descriptive sentence like *The dolphins look like graceful streaks of gray as they glide through the water*. I could also write it so my reader imagines what it's like to be a dolphin by writing *Imagine living underwater even though you need to breathe air. That's what dolphins do*."

Use the students' suggestions to write several possible opening sentences for your piece. You might try writing some sentences that are similar to the ones the students explored in Step 2.

 4 ▶ Quick-Write: Possible Opening Sentences

Ask partners to reread the sections they have written so far. After a moment, use "Think, Pair, Share" to have partners first think about and then discuss:

 Q *What opening sentences might you write to introduce your animal and to capture your readers' attention?* [pause] *Turn to your partner.*

After partners have had a chance to talk, signal for their attention. Have them open to the next blank page in their notebooks and do a 5-minute quick-write together in which they write at least three different ways they could begin their piece.

After 5 minutes, signal for the students' attention and have a few volunteers share a possible opening sentence with the class.

Explain that partners may use one of the opening sentences they just wrote to begin their piece, or they may write another one. Encourage them to keep working until they agree on an opening that they believe will capture their readers' attention.

 5 ▶ Discuss How Partners Will Work Together

Explain and write the following tasks on the board:

- Add a strong opening to your piece.

- Draft your informational piece, planning for any illustrations.

- Share the work fairly.

Ask partners to spend a few minutes deciding what they will work on today and how they will share the work fairly. When they are ready, have them begin working.

WRITING TIME

 Draft Informational Pieces

Have partners work together on their informational pieces. As they work, circulate, observe, and offer assistance. When pairs seem to be working independently, confer with one pair at a time.

TEACHER CONFERENCE NOTE

Continue to confer with pairs about their informational piece. Ask partners to read their drafts aloud and to tell you their plan for their piece. Ask questions such as:

Q *What interesting things have you learned about your animal? Read me your note about that.*

Q *What else do you want to know about your animal? Where will you look for that information?*

Q *Have you found answers to any of your questions? Tell me about them.*

Q *How are your sharing the work fairly?*

Q *Do you think your opening will capture your reader's attention? Why or why not? How might you revise it to be more [scary/interesting/exciting]?*

Document your observations for each pair using the "Conference Notes" record sheet (BLM1).

Signal to let the students know when writing time is over.

SHARING AND REFLECTING

 Share Opening Sentences and Reflect

Explain that each pair will read its opening sentence aloud to the class. Give pairs a moment to decide which partner will read their opening sentence aloud. Go around the room and have each pair read its opening sentence, without comment.

When all pairs have shared a sentence, ask and briefly discuss:

Q *What opening sentences did you hear that captured your attention?*

Q *What ideas did you get about your own opening sentences from hearing others people's openings?*

Explain that pairs will continue to analyze and revise their informational pieces tomorrow.

Day 3

Analyzing and Revising Drafts

In this lesson, the students:

- Check their drafts for interest, order, and completeness

- Finish drafting their informational piece

- Share the work fairly

- Work responsibly in pairs

- Discuss and solve problems that arise in their work together

Materials

- Completed draft of your informational piece from Week 4 (see "Do Ahead" on page 455)

- Loose, lined paper for writing drafts

- Chart paper and a marker

GETTING READY TO WRITE

▶1 Model Analyzing and Revising a Draft

Gather the class with partners sitting together, facing you. Ask them to bring pencils and the drafts of their informational pieces with them. Explain that today partners will reread their drafts to see what they need to add or change to improve them.

Direct the students' attention to your charted draft. Explain that you want to check three things about your draft today. Write the following items on a sheet of chart paper as you say them aloud:

> - Order: Does the order of information make sense? How might I change it?
>
> - Interest: What might I change to better capture my reader's interest?
>
> - Completeness: What more do I need to add so the piece gives enough information about the animal?

◀ **Teacher Note**

Some students may not be done with their draft at this point. This is to be expected. Ask all of the students to pay attention to the lesson so they will know what to do when they are ready.

Explain that you would like the students' feedback to help you revise your draft. Ask them to think about these three things as you read your draft aloud.

Teacher Note

You might say, "I originally thought I would write about the dolphin's physical characteristics first, but it might make more sense to put the information about their habitat first so the reader knows where they are found in the world."

 Use "Think, Pair, Share" to discuss each of these three aspects. Revise your draft based on the students' suggestions and your own thinking.

2▶ Analyze Their Own Drafts

Ask partners to silently read their drafts, thinking about the three questions related to order, interest, and completeness. Once most pairs have finished reading, ask partners to talk with each other about their thinking, discussing the changes and additions that they might make.

After a few minutes, signal for the students' attention and discuss:

Q *What did you and your partner discuss about the order of the information in your piece?*

Q *What do you plan to add to your draft? Why?*

3▶ Discuss How Partners Will Work Together

Explain that today partners will continue to draft their informational piece, making the changes and additions they've discussed. Ask partners to spend a few minutes discussing what they want to accomplish today and how they will share the work. When they are ready, have them return to their seats.

WRITING TIME

4▶ Finish Drafting Informational Pieces

Have partners work together for 20–30 minutes to complete their drafts, making the changes and additions they discussed.

Circulate, observe, and offer assistance. When pairs seem to be working independently, confer with one pair at a time.

TEACHER CONFERENCE NOTE

Continue to confer with pairs about their informational piece. Ask partners to read their drafts aloud and to tell you their plan for their piece. Ask questions such as:

Q *What interesting things you have learned about your animal? Read me your note about that.*

Q *What else do you want to know about your animal? Where will you look for that information?*

Q *Have you found answers to any of your questions? Tell me about them.*

Q *How are your sharing the work fairly?*

Q *Do you think your opening will capture your reader's attention? Why or why not? How might you revise it to be more [scary/interesting/exciting]?*

Q *What will you [write to make this more interesting/change so the order makes more sense/add so that it is more complete]?*

Document your observations for each pair using the "Conference Notes" record sheet (BLM1).

Signal to let the students know when writing time is over.

SHARING AND REFLECTING

 Reflect on Partner Work

Ask and briefly discuss:

Q *How did you and your partner take responsibility for your own parts of the work today?*

Q *What problems did you have? What will you do tomorrow to avoid those problems?*

Explain that pairs will get feedback about their informational pieces from another pair tomorrow.

Day 4

Materials

- Completed draft of your informational piece
- Chart paper and a marker
- *Assessment Resource Book*

Group Conferring

In this lesson, the students:

- Ask for and receive feedback about their writing
- Give feedback in a helpful way
- Ask one another questions about their writing
- Discuss and solve problems that arise in their work together
- Include one another and contribute to group work

GETTING READY TO WRITE

1 ### Prepare for Group Conferences

Explain that today each pair will meet with another pair to confer about their informational pieces (see "Do Ahead" on page 455). They will share their drafts and get feedback from the other pair about anything confusing or unclear; then they will make any necessary revisions until they are convinced that their pieces make sense and are complete.

Remind the students that in the writing community the goal of giving feedback is to help each person create the best possible piece of writing. In pairs and then as a class, discuss:

 Q *What have you learned about giving feedback respectfully? Turn to your partner.*

Q *What problems can arise when giving feedback? How will you avoid those problems today?*

2 ▶ Prepare to Give Feedback: Does It All Make Sense?

Explain that, as the students listen to one another's writing, you would like them to ask themselves the three questions that follow. Write the questions on a sheet of chart paper as you say them aloud:

- Does this writing make sense? Can I track what the author is saying?

- Is there anywhere I am confused? Where?

- What have I heard in this piece that makes me curious?

Help the students practice giving feedback about these three questions by showing your model informational piece and reading it aloud, along with any revisions. Use "Think, Pair, Share" to have partners consider and discuss the three questions about your draft. Then have several volunteers give you feedback about your draft using the three questions.

Encourage the students to listen carefully to their group members and to be ready to report the feedback they heard to the class.

3 ▶ Confer in Groups

Have pairs move into the groups you have assigned. Give them ample time to confer.

CLASS ASSESSMENT NOTE

Circulate among conferring groups and observe the conferences. Ask yourself:

- Are groups staying on task, reading and discussing their writing?

- Are group members asking each other questions about their drafts?

- Are they giving each other feedback in a helpful and respectful way?

Make note of any problems you notice groups having to bring up during the reflection discussion.

Record your observations in the *Assessment Resource Book*.

When most groups have had time to discuss their drafts, call for the class's attention.

4▸ Reflect on Feedback Received

Ask and briefly discuss as a class:

Q *What did the members of your group do to be respectful during your conference?*

Remind the students that when authors receive feedback they may or may not agree with all of it. Authors decide which feedback they will use. Use "Think, Pair, Share" to have partners first think about and then discuss:

 Q *What feedback did you hear today that you might use when you rewrite your draft?* [pause] *Turn to your partner.*

 Q *What feedback do you want to think more about before deciding whether to use it or not?* [pause] *Turn to your partner.*

Discuss How Partners Will Work Together

Explain that today partners will work together to make any agreed-upon revisions and reread their drafts to make sure it is as clear, interesting, and complete as it can be.

Ask partners to spend a few minutes deciding what they will work on today and how they will share the work. When they are ready, have them return to their seats and begin working.

WRITING TIME

Finish Drafts

Have pairs work on finishing their drafts. As they work, circulate, observe, and offer assistance. When pairs seem to be working independently, confer with pairs.

> ### TEACHER CONFERENCE NOTE
>
> Continue to confer with pairs about their informational piece. Ask partners to read their drafts aloud and to tell you their plan for their piece. Ask questions such as:
>
> **Q** *What interesting things have you learned about your animal? Read me your note about that.*
>
> **Q** *What else do you want to know about your animal? Where will you look for that information?*
>
> **Q** *Have you found answers to any of your questions? Tell me about them.*
>
> **Q** *How are your sharing the work fairly?*
>
> **Q** *Do you think your opening will capture your reader's attention? Why or why not? How might you revise it to be more [scary/interesting/exciting]?*
>
> *continues*

> **TEACHER CONFERENCE NOTE** *continued*
>
> **Q** *What will you [write to make this more interesting/change so the order makes more sense/add so that it is more complete]?*
>
> Document your observations for each pair using the "Conference Notes" record sheet (BLM1).

Signal to let the students know when writing time is over.

SHARING AND REFLECTING

 Briefly Reflect on Writing

Help the students reflect on their work today by briefly discussing:

Q *What feedback did you incorporate into your draft today? Tell us about it.*

Explain that pairs will publish their final version next week.

Teacher Note

If many pairs still need time to finish writing their drafts, give them an opportunity to do this before moving on to Week 6.

EXTENSION

Teach Cooperative Structures for Group Work

Look for opportunities throughout the school day for students to work in groups of four (or three or five, if necessary). Two cooperative structures you can teach them to use in group work are "Heads Together" and "Group Brainstorming." These are described in the front matter of volume 1 on page xiv. Group work can be more challenging for students than pair work. Take time to discuss problems, as well as how group members are including one another and contributing responsibly to the work.

Week 6 Overview

GENRE: EXPOSITORY NONFICTION

Writing Focus

- Students write a table of contents.

- Students proofread for spelling, grammar, and punctuation errors.

- Students write final versions of their informational pieces.

- Students present their informational piece to the class from the Author's Chair.

- Students confer with one another and the teacher.

Social Focus

- Students make decisions and solve problems respectfully.

- Students act in fair and caring ways.

- Students express interest in and appreciation for one another's writing.

- Students give their full attention to the person who is speaking.

DO AHEAD

- Prior to Day 1, decide how pairs will publish their final version for the class library. For example, each pair might make a book (see the note on pages 164–165 in volume 1 for bookmaking resources) or make a poster with the final version attached to it. Gather any necessary materials.

- Prior to Day 1, decide whether you will have the students handwrite or use a computer to generate their final versions. You may want to recruit parents or older students to help with word processing and printing.

- Prior to Day 1, locate books with tables of contents in your collection of books about animals to show as examples.

Day 1

Materials

- *Reptiles* from Week 1
- Other books about animals with tables of contents (see "Do Ahead" on page 471)
- Loose, lined paper for final versions
- Unlined paper for illustrations
- (Optional) Computers for word processing
- *Assessment Resource Book*

Writing Final Versions

In this lesson, the students:

- Write the final version of their piece
- Explore and develop a table of contents
- Reach agreement before making decisions
- Share the work fairly

GETTING READY TO WRITE

 Explore Tables of Contents

Gather the class with partners sitting together, facing you. Explain that this week they will work on the final version of their informational piece. They will publish it, share it with the class from the Author's Chair, and place it in the class library.

Remind the students that the purpose of their informational piece is to help their classmates become interested in, and curious about, the animals they selected to research. Explain that authors spark their readers' curiosity and help them know what is in their book by providing a table of contents. Show and read aloud the "Table of Contents" on page 3 of *Reptiles*. Ask and briefly discuss:

Q *What do you notice about how this table of contents is organized?*

Q *How might this table of contents help a reader?*

Point out that the table of contents in *Reptiles* lists the headings for each chapter of the book, as well as some special features such as where to find out more about reptiles, important words used in the book, and information about the author.

Show the tables of contents in several of the other books in your collection and discuss how they are organized. Note that some use the title "Table of Contents," while others use "Contents." Point out that chapter headings are listed in the order they appear in the book along with their page numbers, and special features are listed at the end.

Explain that partners will work together to include a table of contents with their informational piece. Use "Think, Pair, Share" to have partners first think about and then discuss:

 Q *What chapter headings might you and your partner include in your table of contents?* [Pause] *Turn to your partner.*

Signal for attention and have a few pairs share their thinking with the class.

2 ▶ Discuss How Partners Will Work Together

Explain the following tasks as you write them on the board:

- Begin writing your final version.
- Place your sections in the proper order.
- Discuss and write a table of contents.
- Add illustrations and captions.

Ask partners to spend a few minutes deciding what they will accomplish and how they will share the work fairly. Remind them that both partners are responsible for writing sections of the final piece. When they are ready, have them return to their seats and begin working.

WRITING TIME

3 ▶ Write Final Versions and a Table of Contents

Have partners work on the final versions of their informational pieces. As they work, circulate, and observe.

CLASS ASSESSMENT NOTE

Observe pairs working and ask yourself:

* Are partners working together fairly to write a final version of their informational piece?

* Are they including a table of contents?

Support struggling pairs by asking them questions such as:

Q *What are each of you responsible for accomplishing during this writing time?*

Q *Is the way you are sharing the work fair? Why or why not? What can you do to make it so you are sharing the work fairly?*

Q *Why is it important that both of you do your part of the work on this project?*

Record your observations in the *Assessment Resource Book.*

Signal to let the students know when writing time is over.

SHARING AND REFLECTING

 Reflect and "Preview" Pieces as a Class

Explain that each pair will give the class a "preview" of their informational piece by reading any two sentences aloud from it. Ask partners to quietly reread their piece and select two interesting sentences (one for each partner) to read aloud. Give them a few moments to select their sentences then ask the class to listen carefully to one another's sentences and to think about which ones make them curious.

Go around the room and have the students read their sentences aloud, without comment. When all have read, ask and briefly discuss:

Q *What sentences did you hear that made you curious?*

Remind the students that they will hear one another's completed pieces from the Author's Chair later this week. Explain that pairs will continue to work on their final versions tomorrow.

Day 2

Writing Final Versions and Proofreading

In this lesson, the students:

- Proofread for spelling, grammar, and punctuation
- Explore using commas in a series
- Explore using apostrophes to show possession
- Listen for periods as they read their draft aloud
- Work on their final version for publication

GETTING READY TO WRITE

 Briefly Review

Gather the class with partners sitting together, facing you. Explain that today partners will work on finishing the final version of their informational piece. Remind the students that the purpose of these informational pieces is to help their classmates become interested in, and curious about, the animals they selected to research. Explain that their pieces need to be as correct as possible so their classmates can read and understand them easily. Today they will proofread their pieces to make sure they have corrected all of the errors.

 Proofreading: Listening for Periods and Exploring Punctuation

Show the transparencies of "Unpunctuated Nonfiction Passage" (1 and 2) on the overhead projector. Explain that these passages come from books the students have heard, but the passages have been written without punctuation or capitalization. Ask the students to follow along and listen carefully as you read the first passage aloud. Read without pauses. Ask:

Q *What's strange about the way I read this passage?*

Materials

- *A Pack of Wolves* from Week 1
- *Into the Sea* from Week 2
- Transparencies of "Unpunctuated Nonfiction Passages" (1 and 2) (BLM20–BLM21)
- Overhead pen
- *Student Writing Handbook* pages 13–14, and the word bank and proofreading notes sections
- Loose, lined paper for final versions
- Unlined paper for illustrations
- *Assessment Resource Book*

Point out that the passage doesn't sound right because it reads as one long sentence. Ask the students to open to *Student Writing Handbook* page 13, where the passage is reproduced. Have them slowly reread the passage aloud with you, stopping at each place where it feels natural to do so. At each stop (and as appropriate), discuss and model writing a comma or a period and ask the students to do the same. Ask and briefly discuss:

Q *What suggestions do you have for punctuating the phrase "including whimpers, growls, barks, whines, and pants?"*

Q Wolfs, *as it is written here, is not a word in the English language. What do we need to do to this word to make it correct?*

Point out that one way commas are used in sentences is to separate items in a list. Explain that every item in a list is followed by a comma except the last item, which has the word *and* before it (for example, *They make many sounds, including whimpers, growls, barks, whines, and pants…*). Also point out that apostrophes are used to show that something belongs to someone or something else (for example, *A wolf's most famous sound is the howl*).

Show page 20 of *A Pack of Wolves* and explain how the author punctuated this passage.

Ask the students to read the next passage on *Student Writing Handbook* page 14 to themselves. Have them work in pairs to punctuate the passage, listening for the natural ends of sentences, separating items in a series with commas, and adding any other needed punctuation or capitalization. After a few moments, signal for their attention and have volunteers share how they corrected the paragraph. Use the students' suggestions to edit the paragraph on the transparency.

Show page 30 of *Into the Sea* and explain how the author punctuated this passage.

Have the students turn to the proofreading notes section of their *Student Writing Handbooks*. Write the notes in the following diagram where everyone can see them and have the students copy them into their proofreading notes.

Teacher Note

To provide your students with more practice with using commas in a series and using apostrophes to show possession, do the related activities in the *Skill Practice Teaching Guide* with them.

Rule	Example	Notes
Commas in a list	whimpers, growls, barks, whines, and pants	all items have a comma except the last one, which has the word <u>and</u> before it
Apostrophes to show belonging	A wolf's most famous sound is the howl	Use an apostrophe to show that something belongs to someone or something else

 ## Review Using the Word Bank and Proofreading Notes

Remind the students that they should use their word bank and proofreading notes to help them proofread their drafts for spelling and correctness. Briefly review these procedures by reminding the students to:

- Circle words in their draft that they are unsure how to spell, and look them up in their word bank. Add any words that are not already in their word bank after looking them up in a dictionary or other source.

- Use their proofreading notes as a list of things to check in their draft before publishing. Correct any errors by crossing out the error in the draft and writing the correction next to it.

Remind the students to correct any misspellings or errors they may have copied into their final versions yesterday.

 ## Discuss How Partners Will Work Together

Explain the following tasks as you write them on the board:

- Reread your draft aloud and check for correct sentence punctuation.

- Proofread for spelling, using the word bank.

- Proofread for correctness, using the proofreading notes.

- Finish writing your final version, including illustrations and captions.

Ask partners to spend a few minutes deciding what they will work on today and how they will share the work fairly. When they are ready, have them return to their seats and begin working.

WRITING TIME

5▶ Proofread and Write Final Versions

Have pairs work on proofreading and writing their final versions. As they work, circulate, observe, and offer assistance.

> ### CLASS ASSESSMENT NOTE
>
> Observe pairs working and ask yourself:
>
> - Are partners working together fairly to write a final version of their informational piece?
>
> - Are they catching and correcting spelling, grammar, and punctuation errors?
>
> Support struggling pairs by asking them questions such as:
>
> **Q** *What are each of you responsible for accomplishing during this writing time?*
>
> **Q** *Is the way you are sharing the work fair? Why or why not?*
>
> **Q** *What can you do so that you are sharing the work fairly?*
>
> **Q** *Why is it important that both of you do your part of the work on this project?*
>
> Record your observations in the *Assessment Resource Book.*

Signal to let the students know when writing time is over.

SHARING AND REFLECTING

6▶ Reflect on Proofreading

Ask and briefly discuss:

Q *What words did you find in your word bank today? How did you check on words that were not in the word bank?*

Q *What corrections did you make in your draft after reviewing your proofreading notes?*

Explain that the students will finish their pieces tomorrow and begin sharing them from the Author's Chair.

Day 3

Materials

- Materials for publishing informational pieces (see "Do Ahead" on page 471)
- Two chairs to use for Author's Chair sharing

Writing Final Versions and Publishing

In this lesson, the students:

- Publish their informational pieces
- Handle materials responsibly and share them fairly
- Make decisions about how they will present their pieces from the Authors' Chairs
- Express interest in and appreciation for one another's writing
- Ask one another questions about their writing

GETTING READY TO WRITE

 Discuss Handling and Sharing Materials

Have partners sit together at desks today. Explain that pairs will continue publishing their informational pieces and will begin sharing them from the Authors' Chairs today.

Explain the procedure you would like pairs to follow to publish their pieces. Discuss how the students will share materials and equipment fairly and handle them responsibly. Ask and briefly discuss:

Q *What will you do to take care of our [book-making] materials? Why is that important?*

Q *What have you been doing to share equipment like the computer or the hole-punch? Has that been fair? If not, what can we do today to share those things more fairly?*

Discuss How Partners Will Work Together

Explain that today partners will work to finish publishing their piece. They will then decide how they will present their piece to the class (for example, decide what sections each partner will read aloud and practice their presentations). Briefly discuss:

Q *What are some ways partners might share the presentation of their piece?*

Explain that the pairs who finish the publication process today will begin sharing their pieces from the Authors' Chairs. Tell the students that writing time will be a bit shorter to allow time for this sharing. Ask partners to spend a few minutes deciding what they will accomplish and how they will share their work today.

WRITING TIME

 Publish Pieces and Prepare to Share

Have the pairs work on publishing their informational pieces for 15–20 minutes. Circulate, observe, and offer assistance.

Signal to let the students know when writing time is over.

SHARING AND REFLECTING

▶ **Review Sharing Writing from the Author's Chair**

Gather the class with partners sitting together, facing the Authors' Chairs. If necessary, remind them of the procedure you established for presenting books from the Authors' Chairs (see Unit 2, Week 3, Day 4, pages 170–172).

Before asking a pair to share from the Authors' Chairs today, discuss how the students will act, both as presenting authors and as members of the audience.

Teacher Note

If necessary, write today's task on the board where everyone can see them.

 Note

Support trios as necessary to make sure that all three students in each trio have a role in presenting their piece to the class.

Ask and discuss:

Q *Why is it important to speak in a loud, clear voice when you're reading your piece to the class?*

Q *If you're in the audience and you can't hear the author, how can you politely let him or her know?*

Q *How will you let the authors know that you're interested in their piece? Why is it important to express interest in one another's writing?*

Encourage the students to be attentive and considerate audience members. Tell them that you will check in with them afterward to see how they did.

▶5 Conduct Author's Chair Sharing

Ask a pair who has finished publishing its informational piece to read the piece aloud from the Authors' Chairs. At the end of the sharing, facilitate a discussion using questions like those that follow and give the authors an opportunity to respond to the class's comments and questions:

Q *What did you learn about [condors] from hearing [Dante and Thuy's] piece?*

Q *What are you curious about after hearing their piece?*

Q *What questions can we ask [Dante and Thuy] about their piece?*

Follow this procedure and have other pairs share from Authors' Chairs as time permits.

▶6 Reflect on Audience Behavior During Author's Chair Sharing

Ask and briefly discuss:

Q *What did we do well as an audience today? What might we want to work on the next time authors share their work?*

Q *If you shared a piece today, how did the audience make you feel?*
What did they do that made you feel [relaxed/nervous/proud]?

Place the informational pieces in the class library after they are read aloud so students can read them on their own during independent reading time. Explain that tomorrow pairs who have not finished publishing will have time to do so and that more pairs will share their piece from the Authors' Chairs.

EXTENSION

Technology Tip: Publishing Student Writing Online

This week the students are publishing their nonfiction for the class library. Some students might also be interested in publishing their writing online. There are a number of websites where students can publish their writing online; search for them using the keywords "publishing children's writing." Publishing online allows family members and friends to easily access and enjoy students' writing.

Day 4

Materials

- Materials for publishing informational pieces
- Two chairs to use for Author's Chair sharing

Writing Final Versions and Publishing

In this lesson, the students:

- Review and reflect on writing nonfiction
- Finish publishing their pieces
- Present their pieces from the Authors' Chairs
- Express interest in and appreciation for one another's writing
- Ask one another questions about their writing
- Give their full attention to the person who is speaking

GETTING READY TO WRITE

1 ▸ Review and Reflect on Writing Nonfiction

Have partners sit together at desks today. Remind the students that over the past six weeks they have learned about writing nonfiction and have researched and written a nonfiction piece about an animal they were curious about. Ask:

Q *What have you learned about writing nonfiction over the past weeks?*

> **Students might say:**
>
> "I learned that you can write about things your are curious about."
>
> "I agree with [Brad]. I learned that you can find out about things by researching them."
>
> "In addition to what [Jackie] said, I learned that you can take notes and use them in your nonfiction writing."
>
> "I learned ways to capture the reader's attention and make the reader curious about my topic."

FACILITATION TIP

Reflect on your experience over the past weeks with **pacing class discussions**. Do the pacing techniques feel comfortable and natural to you? Do you find yourself using them throughout the school day? What effect has your focus on pacing had on your students' participation in discussions? We encourage you to continue to think about how to pace class discussions throughout the year.

Have partners use "Think, Pair, Share" to first think about and then discuss each of the following questions:

 Q *What was your favorite part of working on your informational piece?* [pause] *Turn to your partner.*

 Q *What is one thing you are glad you learned about writing nonfiction?* [pause] *Turn to your partner.*

 Q *What did you find challenging about writing nonfiction?* [pause] *Turn to your partner.*

Remind the students that writers become better over time as they practice writing again and again. Encourage students who feel drawn to nonfiction to continue to research and write about nonfiction topics they are interested in during their free time and during the open weeks of this program.

Explain that today partners finish publishing their piece and then decide and practice how they will present it to the class. Those who finish may write anything they choose during writing time.

Explain that after writing time, more pairs will share their pieces with the class from the Authors' Chairs. Ask partners to spend a few minutes deciding what they will accomplish and how they will share their work today.

WRITING TIME

 Finish Publishing Pieces and Prepare to Share

Have pairs work on publishing and preparing to share for 10–15 minutes. Circulate, observe, and offer assistance.

Signal to let the students know when writing time is over.

SHARING AND REFLECTING

 Conduct Author's Chair Sharing

Gather the class with partners sitting together, facing the Authors' Chairs. Remind them to speak in a loud, clear voice and to show interest in and appreciation for their classmates' writing.

Have a pair read its piece aloud from the Authors' Chairs. At the end of the sharing, facilitate a discussion using questions like those that follow, and give the authors an opportunity to respond to the class's comments and questions:

Q *What did you learn about [how bears hibernate] from hearing [Cara and Tomas's] piece?*

Q *What are you curious about after hearing their piece?*

Q *What questions can we ask [Cara and Tomas] about their piece?*

Repeat this procedure to have other pairs share from the Authors' Chairs as time permits.

Assure the students that pairs who haven't yet shared will get to share their published informational piece from the Authors' Chairs in the coming days.

After the informational pieces are read aloud, place them in the class library so students can read them during independent reading time.

Teacher Note

If necessary, repeat today's lesson for a few more days, or even another week, to give all the pairs time to finish publishing their pieces (see "Open Weeks" in the volume 1 front matter on page xvi). Students who finish may begin a new piece of writing (nonfiction or otherwise) or continue working on a piece of writing they started earlier.

Even if you decide to begin another genre unit immediately, continue to have pairs share their nonfiction informational pieces from the Authors' Chairs until everyone has had a chance to do so.

4 **Reflect on Interactions and Thank One Another**

Ask and briefly discuss:

Q *What did we do well as an audience today? What do we still want to work on the next time authors share their work?*

Q *If you shared a piece today, how did the audience make you feel? What did they do that made you feel [relaxed/nervous/proud]?*

Point out that partners have worked closely together for several weeks to research and write about the animal they chose. Ask and briefly discuss:

Q *In what ways did you and your partner help each other on this project?*

 Q *What do you appreciate about how your partner worked with you? Turn and tell your partner.*

Ask partners to take a moment to thank each other for their help and collaboration.

Teacher Note

This is the last week of the expository nonfiction unit. You will need to reassign partners before beginning the next unit.

EXTENSION

Write Letters Home About Nonfiction

Provide letter-writing practice for the students by having them write a letter home about what they learned about nonfiction from working on their animal pieces. Discuss questions such as:

Q *What's special about nonfiction writing?*

Q *What steps did you and your partner go through to research and write about your animal?*

Q *What is one thing you're proud of about your published informational piece?*

If necessary, review the elements of a letter (date, salutation, body, closing, and signature) by modeling or writing a shared sample letter with the class. Have the students write and proofread their letters; then attach each student's letter to a copy of the published informational piece he helped to write and send it home.

Genre

Functional Writing

Functional Writing

Functional Writing

During this three-week unit, the students explore functional writing. They read and discuss directions for how to do things, explore craft elements of functional writing, and write directions for others to follow. As the students write, they consider the audience and purpose and review for sequence, accuracy and completeness. The students frequently work with a partner during the unit. They reach agreement and make decisions together, work responsibly, share the work and materials fairly, and give and receive feedback respectfully.

Development Across the Grades

Grade	Nonfiction Topics	Craft Focus	Skills and Conventions
3	• Writing directions for how to take care of something, draw something, and do a craft project	• Writing with an audience and purpose in mind	• Checking directions for sequence, completeness, accuracy, and clarity
4	• Writing directions for recipes, cartoon drawings, and games	• Writing with an audience and purpose in mind	• Checking directions for sequence, completeness, accuracy, and clarity

UNIT OVERVIEW

WEEK	DAY 1	DAY 2	DAY 3	DAY 4
	Immersion and Drafting			
1	**Exploring Functional Writing:** *Kittens* **Quick-Write:** Ideas about things they take care of	**Exploring Functional Writing:** *My Pet Puppy* **Focus:** Write about how to take care of something	**Exploring Functional Writing:** *1-2-3 Draw Ocean Life* **Quick-Write:** Ideas about things they know how to do	**Exploring Functional Writing** **Focus:** Writing directions for a sketch
2	**Exploring Functional Writing** **Focus:** Exploring sequence of directions	**Exploring Functional Writing:** "Puzzle Sticks" **Focus:** Exploring completeness in directions	**Selecting Topics** **Focus:** Writing directions for an activity they know how to do	**Drafting and Revising** **Focus:** Revising game directions; exploring accuracy and clarity
	Revision, Proofreading, and Publication			
3	**Group Conferring and Revising** **Focus:** Conferring about directions; revising if necessary	**Proofreading** **Focus:** Punctuation, grammar, spelling; writing final versions	**Publishing** **Focus:** Author's Chair sharing	**Publishing** **Focus:** Reflecting on functional writing; Author's Chair sharing

GENRE: FUNCTIONAL WRITING

Kittens
by Niki Walker and Bobbie Kalman
(Crabtree Publishing, 2004)

Well-organized text and photographs explain how to choose and raise a kitten.

My Pet Puppy
by Marilyn Baillie
(Kids Can Press, 2005)

Methods of puppy care are described using a notebook format.

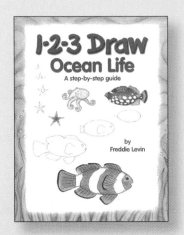

1-2-3 Draw Ocean Life
by Freddie Levin
(Peel Productions, 2005)

This book of easy-to-follow drawing instructions explores sea life.

Writing Focus

- Students hear, read, and discuss functional writing.

- Students explore how information is communicated in functional writing.

- Students list ideas for functional writing.

- Students discuss, follow, and write directions.

Social Focus

- Students listen respectfully to the thinking of others and share their own.

- Students work in a responsible way.

DO AHEAD

- Prior to Day 1, decide how you will randomly assign partners to work together during this unit. See the front matter for suggestions about assigning partners randomly (page xiii) and for considerations for pairing English Language Learners (page xxviii).

- Prior to Day 1, collect functional writing such as cookbooks, recipes, online maps with directions, and books about how to make or do things. If possible, include some books about how to draw different things like animals and cartoon characters. Search for titles online using the keywords "children's drawing books."

- Prior to Day 1, think about the procedure you use for gathering the class with partners sitting together, facing you. Write these directions, as simply as possible, on a chart (see example on page 497).

- Prior to Day 2, identify things in the classroom that the students help to take care of (for example, a plant, a fish, or the art center). Pick one to use in "Shared Writing" on this day.

- Prior to Day 4, draw a simple sketch of any kind of animal on a sheet of chart paper, leaving room to write directions for drawing it. Make the drawing very simple, requiring no more than five steps (see the example on page 509).

TEACHER AS WRITER

Have you asked yourself lately: "When was the last time I saw something for the first time?"
— *Cecilia Borromeo*

Most of us are surrounded by, and rely on, functional writing, or written language that helps us function in modern society. This week join your students in beginning to explore functional writing by making a list of all the functional writing you encounter daily, including that which you read and that which you write yourself. Think about directions, signs, lists, flyers, online text, and other sources of information.

Day 1

Materials

- *Kittens*
- Chart with directions for gathering (see "Do Ahead" on page 495)
- Collection of functional writing (see "Do Ahead" on page 495)

Exploring Functional Writing

In this lesson, the students:

- Work with a new partner
- Hear, read, and discuss functional writing
- Explore how information is communicated in functional writing
- Quick-write ideas about things they take care of
- Share what they learn about their partner
- Handle materials responsibly

About Teaching Functional Writing

The purpose of functional writing, like all nonfiction, is to inform. While expository nonfiction provides information about a topic (for example, the animals of New Zealand), functional nonfiction explains how to do something (for example, how to brush your teeth, use a washing machine, or build a rocket). Functional writing also helps people with daily living (for example, lists, labels, menus, and schedules).

The goals of this unit are to introduce the students to functional writing, help them think about functional writing craft elements, and provide opportunities for them to do functional writing. There are two phases to this unit: Immersion and Drafting (two weeks), and Revision, Proofreading, and Publication (one week). During the first phase, the students explore and try their hand at functional writing. In the second phase, they write directions for a game and make a class book.

GETTING READY TO WRITE

Teacher Note

The partners you assign today will stay together for the unit.

Making Meaning® Teacher

Either have the students work with their current *Making Meaning* partner or assign them a new partner for this unit.

 1 ▸ **Pair Students and Introduce Functional Writing**

Randomly assign partners (see "Do Ahead" on page 495) and make sure they know each other's names. Signal for their attention; then, without speaking, point to the chart with the directions for gathering. Give the students a moment to read the directions. Then signal for them to silently follow the directions.

> Directions:
>
> 1. When I point to your table, gather your writing notebooks and pencils.
>
> 2. Quietly get up and push in your chairs.
>
> 3. Walk to the rug area.
>
> 4. Sit next to your partner, facing me.

Once the class has gathered with partners sitting together, ask:

Q *How was following my written directions different from following my directions when I say them aloud?*

Explain that written directions are a form of *functional writing*—writing that helps people learn how to do things and live their lives. In addition to directions and instructions, functional writing includes such things as menus, lists, recipes, schedules, and telephone books. Explain that during this unit the students will explore one type of functional writing—writing that gives directions for how to do something.

◀ **Teacher Note**

As you discuss different types of functional writing, you might show some examples from your functional writing collection.

Have partners get to know each other by talking about something they know how to do that they could teach someone younger (for example, tie their shoes, throw a ball, or set the table). Ask them to be ready to share their partner's thinking with the class.

After a few minutes, signal for the students' attention and ask:

Q *What can your partner teach someone younger to do?*

▶ ## Read and Discuss Parts of *Kittens*

Show *Kittens* and read the title and the names of the authors (Niki Walker and Bobbie Kalman) aloud. Explain that this book is an example of functional writing and teaches readers how to take care of a kitten. Ask and briefly discuss:

Q *What is something you might need to do to take care of a kitten?*

Explain that you will read parts of the book aloud. Show page 3, "Contents," and read a few of the topics in the book. Read pages 6–7, showing the illustrations, then show and read pages 14–21, clarifying vocabulary as you read. Stop during the reading to point out how information is communicated (for example, the use of headings and text, pictures and captions, and text boxes containing lists and other information that might be useful to the reader).

Teacher Note

To review the procedure for defining vocabulary during the reading, see volume 1, page 45.

Suggested Vocabulary

nutrients: things found in food, such as vitamins, that people and animals need to stay healthy (p. 16)

whiskers: long stiff hairs that grow near the mouths of animals such as cats and dogs (p. 21)

ELL Vocabulary

English Language Learners may benefit from discussing additional vocabulary, including:

frisky: playful (p. 6)

allergic: likely to sneeze, itch, or get a rash because of touching or breathing in something (p. 7)

properly: correctly or in the right way (p. 14)

litter box: box where cats can go to the bathroom indoors (p. 18; refer to the illustrations on pp. 18 and 19)

veterinarian: doctor for animals (p. 21)

Ask and briefly discuss:

Q *What is something you learned from this reading about taking care of a kitten?*

▶ Quick-Write: Things We Take Care Of

Teacher Note

To review the procedure for "Think, Pair, Share," see page xiv.

Use "Think, Pair, Share" to have partners first think about and then discuss:

 Q *What do you know how to take care of that you could write about?* [pause] *Turn to your partner.*

Students might say:

"My bike. I wash it and grease the chain."

"I take care of my neighbor's plants when she's gone. I could write about that."

"I could write about taking care of my little sister."

"I know how to take care of my pet rabbit."

"My teeth!"

Ask the students to open their notebooks to the next blank page in their writing ideas section, label the page "Things I Take Care Of," and list things they know how to take care of that they could write about. After about 5 minutes, signal for the students' attention and have a few volunteers share an idea they wrote with the class. Explain that the students may add to their lists during writing time today.

▶4 Introduce the Collection of Functional Writing

Show the students the collection of functional writing. Point out some of the different types of directions in the collection. Explain that the students may look at the materials in this collection today to find examples of functional writing. Explain any procedures for using the collection, then ask and briefly discuss:

Q *What will you do to handle the materials in our functional writing collections responsibly?*

Tell the students that you will check in with them at the end of the lesson to see how they did with handling the materials responsibly.

WRITING TIME

▶5 Write Independently

Ask the students to return to their seats for 20–30 minutes of silent writing. During this time they may add to their list of things they know how to take care of, browse through the functional writing collection, or write about anything they choose. Remind the students that they should double-space all writing and that there should be no talking, whispering, or walking around during the silent writing time.

ELL Note

If necessary, simplify the question on the previous page by rephrasing it in the following way:

Q *What do you take care of?*

Q *What do you do to take care of that?*

Q *What could you write about that?*

Teacher Note

Note that today the students may do functional writing or write about anything else they choose. On Day 2, after exposure to another example of functional writing, all the students will be asked to begin writing in this genre.

Join the students in writing for a few minutes and then circulate and observe.

Signal to let the students know that writing time is over. Have them return any functional writing they borrowed from the class collection.

SHARING AND REFLECTING

 ### Share Ideas for Writing and Reflect

Gather the class with partners sitting together, facing you. Have partners share with each other what they wrote about today. After a few minutes, signal for the students' attention and ask partners to talk briefly about what they learned about functional writing today. After a few more minutes, signal for the class's attention and discuss:

Q *What is something that you learned about functional writing today?*

Q *What is something that you learned about your partner today?*

Q *What did you do to handle our functional writing materials responsibly?*

Explain that tomorrow the students will continue to explore functional writing.

EXTENSION

Read More from *Kittens*

If the students are interested, read aloud and discuss more sections of *Kittens* with them. Invite students who have experience with kittens or cats to share what they know with the class.

Day 2

Exploring Functional Writing

In this lesson, the students:

- Hear, read, and discuss functional writing
- Explore audience and purpose in functional writing
- Write about how to take care of something
- Speak clearly and listen to one another
- Handle materials responsibly

GETTING READY TO WRITE

 Read and Discuss Parts of *My Pet Puppy*

Gather the class with partners sitting together, facing you. Review that yesterday they began exploring functional writing—writing that helps people learn how to do things and live their lives. Show the cover of *Kittens* and remind them that they heard part of this book. Explain that you will read part of another book about how to take care of a pet.

Show the cover of *My Pet Puppy* and read the title and the author's and illustrator's names. Read pages 2–9, showing the illustrations and discussing the various ways information is presented (for example, text with headings; lists; the "Bow-Wow!" feature with tips, jokes, and things to try; and the Puppy Notebook with places for the reader to write information). Clarify vocabulary as you read.

> **Suggested Vocabulary**
>
> **teething toys:** toys to chew on when new teeth are coming through the gums (p. 6)
>
> **gnaw:** chew (p. 7)

Ask and briefly discuss:

Q   *What have you learned so far about taking care of a puppy?*

Flip through the rest of the book, selecting a few additional pages to read aloud and discuss. Ask and briefly discuss:

Q   *How is this book similar to* Kittens? *How is it different?*

Show pages 16–17 in *Kittens* and point out that, as in *Kittens*, *My Pet Puppy* uses text with headings, pictures with captions, and text boxes containing more detailed information.

2▶ Discuss Audience and Purpose

Explain that authors of functional writing consider several things when writing directions for how to do something. One thing they ask themselves is who they are writing for, or who their audience is. Write the question Who is the audience? on a sheet of chart paper entitled "Writing Good Directions." Ask:

Q   *Who is the audience for* Kittens *and* My Pet Puppy*?*

Q   *Authors write differently depending on whether they are writing for children or adults. What might an author want to do when writing for children?*

Students might say:

"An author would use simpler words for children."

"I think an author needs to explain more things to children."

"Children might need pictures of each step, especially if they are just learning to read."

Point out that authors ask themselves why they are writing the directions, or what their purpose is. If the purpose is to help children successfully take care of a pet, the author will make sure that the information will be clear to a child reading the book.

ELL Note

If necessary, simplify this question by rephrasing it in the following way:

Q   *Adult books have lots of words. What do books for children have in them?*

Shared Writing: How to Take Care of Something in the Classroom

Review that *Kittens* and *My Pet Puppy* are books that tell the reader how to take care of a kitten or puppy. Ask:

 Q *Look around our class. What do we take care of that we could write about? Turn to your partner.*

After a moment, signal for the students' attention and explain that you would like their help in writing directions for how to take care of something in the classroom—for example, the class guinea pig (see "Do Ahead" on page 495). Use "Think, Pair, Share" to have partners first think about and then discuss:

 Q *If we were going to write about how to take care of [our guinea pig], what might we write?* [pause] *Turn to your partner.*

Use the students' suggestions to write directions on a sheet of chart paper. For example:

How to Take Care of Our Guinea Pig

- Change the bedding every day.
- Scrub the cage with hot, soapy water once a week.
- Feed her every morning and evening.
- Change the water every day.
- Put things in the cage for her to chew on, crawl through, and climb on.
- Gently brush her every day.

◀ **Teacher Note**

Record the students' ideas as they state them. Do not worry about sequencing the directions at this point. The students will explore sequencing later in the unit.

Remind the students that yesterday they each generated a list of things they know how to take care of. Explain that today they will add any new ideas to their list and then pick one to write about.

WRITING TIME

4 ▶ Write Independently

Write the following directions on the board:

- Add any new ideas to your list of things you know how to take care of.

- Pick one idea and write about it.

- When finished, browse through the functional writing collection.

Ask the students to return to their seats and work silently for 20–30 minutes. Join them in writing for a few minutes and then walk around the room and observe.

CLASS ASSESSMENT NOTE

Observe the students and ask yourself:

- Do the students start writing quickly and stay on task?

- Are they able to write directions for their chosen topics?

If you notice students having difficulty starting to write after 5–10 minutes, help to stimulate their thinking by asking them questions such as:

Q *What is something you take care of at home?*

Q *If you were going to teach someone else how to take care of that thing, what would you say to do first? How can you write that as a sentence?*

Q *What would you say to do next? How will you write that as a sentence?*

Record your observations in the *Assessment Resource Book*.

Signal to let the students know when writing time is over. Have them return any functional writing they borrowed to the class collection.

SHARING AND REFLECTING

 Reflect on Independent Writing

Ask and briefly discuss:

Q   *What topics did you choose to write about?*

Q   *What is one thing that you wrote about [taking care of your bedroom]? Read us a sentence you wrote about it.*

Q   *What did you discover about writing directions? What was easy? What was hard? Why?*

Explain that tomorrow the students will hear and discuss another example of functional writing.

Teacher Note

Save the "Writing Good Directions" chart for use on Day 3 and throughout the unit.

Day 3

Materials

- *1-2-3 Draw Ocean Life*
- "Writing Good Directions" chart from Day 2
- Transparency of "Dolphin" (BLM22)
- Drawing paper for each student
- Chart paper and a marker
- Collection of functional writing
- (Optional) Collected drawing books (see "Do Ahead" on page 495)

Exploring Functional Writing

In this lesson, the students:

- Explore audience and purpose in functional writing
- Explore directions for drawing
- Quick-write ideas about things they know how to do
- Use writing time responsibly

GETTING READY TO WRITE

 Read Parts of *1-2-3 Draw Ocean Life* and Draw

Have partners sit together at desks today. Remind the students that they have been exploring functional writing and have heard two books about how to take care of something. Explain that today they will hear another example of functional writing—a book that gives directions for how to do something.

Show the cover of *1-2-3 Draw Ocean Life* and read the title and author's name aloud. Show and read "Before you begin" on page 2 aloud. Then show the "Contents" on page 3 and read a few of the topics aloud. Read "Important Drawing Tips" at the bottom of page 3 and continue reading to the bottom of page 4. Skip page 5 and read to the bottom of page 6.

Pointing to the question on the "Writing Good Directions" chart, ask and briefly discuss:

Q *Who is the audience for this book, or who is going to read it?*

Invite the students to join you in trying to draw the dolphin following the directions on page 6. Distribute a sheet of drawing paper to each student and show the transparency of "Dolphin"

Teacher Note

▶ If necessary, point out that the audience for this book is children and the purpose is to teach them how to draw creatures that live in the sea.

using the overhead projector. Read each step aloud, following the directions for drawing the dolphin on a sheet of chart paper while the students follow along on their own papers.

When you and the students have finished drawing, ask and briefly discuss:

Q *What does the author of this book do to help us learn to draw a dolphin?*

Students might say:

"The author numbers the steps so you can do them in order."

"In addition to what [Deborah] said, each step only has a little bit to do. That makes it easier to learn."

"I agree with [Victor]. The drawings also help us see what to do."

2 ▶ **Quick-Write: Things We Know How to Do**

Show the back cover of *1-2-3 Draw Ocean Life* and read the caption under the author's photograph aloud. Point out that author Freddie Levin chose to write a book about drawing because it is something she knows how to do and enjoys. Ask and briefly discuss:

Q *What do you know how to do that you could write about?*

Students might say:

"I can throw a football."

"I know the five ballet positions."

"I can play a game on the computer."

"I can make cookies."

"I know how to change a tire on my bike."

Ask the students to open their notebooks to the next blank page in their writing ideas section, label the page "Things I Know How to Do," and list things they know how to do that they could write about. After about five minutes, signal for their attention and have a few volunteers share an idea with the class. Explain that the students may add to their lists during writing time today.

◀ **Teacher Note**

Regularly remind the students to use the discussion prompts they learned when they participate in class discussions. The prompts are:

- "I agree with _____ because…"
- "I disagree with _____ because…"
- "In addition to what _____ said, I think…"

FACILITATION TIP

During this unit, we encourage you to **avoid repeating or paraphrasing** students' responses. It is easy to habitually repeat what students say when they speak too softly or to paraphrase them when they don't express themselves clearly. This teaches students to listen to you but not necessarily to one another. Try refraining from repeating or paraphrasing and see what happens. Encourage the students to take responsibility by asking one another to speak up or by asking a question if they don't understand what a classmate has said. (See the front matter for special considerations for English Language Learners.)

WRITING TIME

 Write Independently

Write the following choices on the board and have the students work on them for 20–30 minutes.

- Add to your list of things you know how to do.

- Use what you learned today to draw your own pictures.

- Browse through the functional writing collection.

Make *1-2-3 Draw Ocean Life* and any other drawing books you've collected available for interested students to share during the writing time.

Join the students in writing for a few minutes; then circulate, observe, and offer assistance.

Signal to let the students know when writing time is over. Have them return any functional writing they borrowed from the class collection.

SHARING AND REFLECTING

 Reflect on Functional Writing and Working Responsibly

Ask and briefly discuss:

Q *What did you write about today?*

Q *What interesting information did you come across when browsing the functional writing collection? Tell us about it.*

Q *What did you do to work responsibly today? What do you need to work on tomorrow?*

Throughout the discussion, share some of the things that you noticed when observing independent writing.

Explain that tomorrow the students will explore more directions for drawing.

EXTENSION

More Practice Following Drawing Directions

To provide more practice with following drawing directions, repeat today's whole-class drawing activity using transparencies of "Doodle a Zoodle," "Bottlenosed Dolphin," and "Jackrabbit" (BLM23–BLM26). You might facilitate a discussion comparing the two sets of instructions for drawing a dolphin by asking:

Q *Which directions for drawing a dolphin were easier to use? Why do you think so?*

Day 4

Materials

- *1-2-3 Draw Ocean Life* from Day 3
- Charted drawing (see "Do Ahead" on page 495)
- Drawing paper for each student
- Collection of functional writing
- Chart paper and a marker
- *Assessment Resource Book*

Exploring Functional Writing

In this lesson, the students:

- Explore directions for drawing
- Write directions for drawing an animal
- Explore audience and purpose in functional writing
- Share ways they have dealt with challenges in their writing

GETTING READY TO WRITE

 Shared Writing: Write Directions for a Drawing

Have partners sit together at desks today. Show the cover of *1-2-3 Draw Ocean Life* and remind the students that yesterday they learned something about drawing sea creatures from this functional writing book. Explain that today they will have a chance to create their own drawing of an animal and write directions for it. Next week partners will exchange directions and try to draw each other's animals.

Show the animal you drew (see "Do Ahead" on page 495) and explain that you would like the students' help to write directions for drawing it. Write the first step and an accompanying sketch under the drawing (see diagram); then ask:

Q *What direction shall I write next in order to explain how to draw my animal?*

Use the students' suggestions to write the remaining steps for your drawing.

1. Draw an oval for the cat's face.

2. Draw two triangles for the ears and a smaller one for the nose.

3. Draw two short, curved lines on each side of the nose to make whiskers.

4. Draw two ovals with circles inside them for eyes.

5. Draw a curved line for the mouth.

2 ▶ Prepare to Draw Simple Animals

Explain the following directions for writing time as you write them on the board:

- Draw two or three simple animals and then pick one.

- Write directions for drawing that animal. Draw a picture to go with each step.

Ask and briefly discuss:

Q *Who will be your audience, or who will read your directions?*

Q *What do you want your reader to learn?*

If necessary, point out to the students that their partner will be the audience for their directions, and the purpose of the directions is to teach their partner how to draw their animal.

WRITING TIME

3 **Write Independently**

Distribute more drawing paper and have the students work silently for 20–30 minutes. As they work, walk around and observe. If students finish early, they may repeat the activity with another animal or browse the functional writing collection.

CLASS ASSESSMENT NOTE

Observe the students and ask yourself:

* Are the students able to draw a simple animal and write directions for how to draw it?

* Are they able to write directions that others can follow?

Support struggling students by having them describe their animal to you (without you looking at it) and asking:

Q *What is the first thing you do to draw your animal? How can you write that as a sentence?*

Q *What do you do next?*

If you notice many students struggling to write directions, call the class together and model another example as you did in Step 1. Then have the students resume their own writing.

Record your observations in the *Assessment Resource Book*.

Signal to let the students know when writing time is over.

SHARING AND REFLECTING

4 **Briefly Reflect on Challenges**

Ask and briefly discuss:

Q *What was challenging about writing directions for drawing your animal?*

Q *How did other people deal with that challenge?*

Remind the students that next week they will exchange their directions with their partner and try to draw each other's animals.

EXTENSION

Explore More Drawings in *1-2-3 Draw Ocean Life*

Have the students follow the directions on other pages of *1-2-3 Draw Ocean Life*.

Teacher Note

Be sure that all of the students have completed the directions for their drawing before the next lesson.

Week 2 Overview

GENRE: FUNCTIONAL WRITING

Writing Focus

- Students hear, read, and discuss functional writing.

- Students explore sequence and completeness in functional writing.

- Students discuss, follow, and write directions for how to make a puzzle.

Social Focus

- Students make decisions and solve problems respectfully.

- Students act in fair and caring ways.

- Students help one another improve their writing.

DO AHEAD

- Prior to Day 2, make arrangements with a kindergarten or first grade class to receive and try the "Puzzle Stick" puzzles your students will make. If your class has a younger buddy class, this is a great opportunity to share with them.

Day 1

Materials

- "Writing Good Directions" chart from Week 1
- Transparency of "Dolphin" (BLM22)
- Collection of functional writing
- Drawing paper for the students
- "Conference Notes" record sheet for each student (BLM1)

Exploring Functional Writing

In this lesson, the students:

- Explore sequence in functional writing
- Give feedback respectfully
- Revise directions based on partner feedback

GETTING READY TO WRITE

 Discuss Sequence in Functional Writing

Have partners get their animal sketches from last week and sit together at their seats. Remind them that last week they began exploring functional writing that tells how to do things. Direct their attention to the "Writing Good Directions" chart, read the items on the chart, and remind them that they will keep a list of things that authors think about when writing directions.

Show the transparency of "Dolphins" and remind the students that they learned how to draw a dolphin from these directions. Point out that the directions are written in the order that they should be done. Reread directions 1–4 and ask and briefly discuss:

Q *Why does it make sense for the directions to be in this order?*

Q *Would these directions work if they were written in a different order? Why or why not?*

Students might say:

"The order makes sense because you draw the body before drawing the things that go on the body, like the fin."

"It wouldn't work to put shading and coloring on the dolphin first because you wouldn't know where to do it."

Explain that the order, or *sequence*, of information is very important to think about when writing directions. On the "Writing Good Directions" chart, add *Does the order of the directions make sense?*

▶2 Review Drafts for Sequence

Ask the students to read the directions they wrote for drawing their animal, asking themselves the question: *Does the order of the directions make sense?* Have them make any changes to their writing so that they can answer "yes" to this question.

When most of the students have finished making any revisions, signal for their attention. Ask and briefly discuss:

Q *What changes did you make to the order of your directions? Why did you make them?*

▶3 Exchange Directions with Partners

Explain that partners will exchange directions and follow them to draw each other's animals. Ask and briefly discuss:

Q *If you have difficulty following your partner's directions, what might you do?*

Distribute the drawing paper and have partners exchange their directions and follow them. After a few minutes, signal for attention and explain that partners will give each other feedback about their directions. Briefly discuss:

Q *What do you know about how to give feedback respectfully?*

Direct the students' attention back to the question *Does the order of the directions make sense?* on the "Writing Good Directions" chart and encourage partners to give each other feedback about this question.

Allow time for partners to give each other feedback. Then signal for the students' attention. Explain that during writing time today, the students will use their partner's feedback to revise their directions, if necessary.

WRITING TIME

4 ▶ Write Independently

Write the following directions on the board and have the students work silently for 20–30 minutes.

- Think about you partner's feedback and revise your directions, if necessary.

- Write directions for another animal drawing.

- Browse the functional writing collection.

Provide the students with more drawing paper, as needed. When everyone seems to be working independently, begin conferring with individual students.

TEACHER CONFERENCE NOTE

During the coming week, confer with individual students by asking them to show and read you their functional writing. Ask yourself:

- Are the directions clear and easy to follow?

- Does the sequence of the directions make sense?

If possible, try following the student's directions and then probe his thinking by asking questions such as:

Q *I am not clear about how to [draw the eye]. What can you tell me that will help me know what to do? How will you write that in your directions?*

Q *I'm confused about the order of what I'm to do. Do I finish the [petals] before I draw the [stem]? How can you make that clear in your directions?*

Document your observations for each student using the "Conference Notes" record sheet (BLM1). Use the "Conference Notes" records sheets during conferences throughout this unit.

Signal to let the students know when writing time is over.

SHARING AND REFLECTING

▶ **5** **Reflect on Revisions and on Writing Directions**

Briefly discuss:

Q *What changes did you make in your directions based on your partner's feedback?*

Q *What have you learned about how to write good directions?*

Explain that tomorrow the students will explore another example of functional writing.

Day 2

Exploring Functional Writing

In this lesson, the students:

- Explore directions for making a puzzle
- Explore completeness in functional writing
- Make a puzzle and write shared directions for it
- Handle materials responsibly

GETTING READY TO WRITE

 Read and Model "Puzzle Sticks"

Have partners sit together at desks today. Remind the students that they have heard and explored functional writing that tells how to take care of and do things. Explain that today they will explore another example of functional writing that tells how to do something.

Show the transparency of "Puzzle Sticks" and explain that this activity is from a book of craft projects for children. Explain that "Puzzle Sticks" gives directions for making a puzzle that someone else can solve. Read "Puzzle Sticks" aloud and ask the students to watch as you model following the directions to make the puzzle.

After making the puzzle, ask and briefly discuss:

Q *Did the directions give us all the information we needed to make the puzzle? Why or why not?*

Students might say:

"I think the directions give all the information needed to make the puzzle."

"I disagree with [Jeremy]. The materials don't say that you need markers and tape."

"I agree with [Tomas] about the materials, but I think otherwise the directions are good."

Explain that authors of functional writing need to think about whether they have included all the information the reader needs to do the activity. On the "Writing Good Directions" chart, write the question *Does the reader have all of the information needed?*

 Make "Puzzle Sticks"

Explain that each student will follow the "Puzzle Stick" directions to make a puzzle. When all the puzzles are completed, they will give them to a younger class in the school to enjoy (see "Do Ahead" on page 515). Ask and briefly discuss:

Q *We are making these puzzles for our [kindergarten buddies]. What do we need to think about so these puzzles are just right for them?*

Students might say:

"The pictures should be simple."

"We might draw something that would be interesting to them."

"We could use bright colors."

Read the directions aloud once more and keep them projected for students to refer to as they do the activity. Distribute the craft sticks, tape, and markers and have students make their puzzles.

 Exchange and Try Out Puzzles

When the students have finished making their puzzles, signal for attention and explain that partners will exchange and try to solve each other's puzzles. Ask and briefly discuss:

Q *What will you do to handle your partner's puzzle responsibly?*

Have partners exchange puzzles. Give them a few minutes to solve each other's puzzles.

◀ **Teacher Note**

If the students don't mention it, remind them that their drawing should go across all of the sticks so each stick has a part of the drawing on it. This will help younger students know which side of the stick is part of the puzzle.

WRITING TIME

▶ **4** ▶ **Shared Writing: Directions to Accompany Puzzles**

Distribute a rubber band to each student to wrap around their set of puzzle sticks. Ask the students to set their puzzles aside and help you write a set of directions to go with the puzzles to the younger class. The directions should explain how to put the puzzle together. Use "Think, Pair, Share" to have partners first think about and then discuss:

Teacher Note

If the students have difficulty answering this question, suggest ideas like those in the "Students might say" note.

 Q *What information should we include in our directions for putting the puzzle together?* [pause] *Turn to your partner.*

Signal for attention and have a few volunteers share their thinking with the class.

> **Students might say:**
>
> "We should say to lay out the sticks so the colored side is showing."
>
> "We should say to put the sticks together so they make a picture."
>
> "If they want to check if they put the puzzle together right, we can tell them to turn the sticks over to check the numbers."

Ask and briefly discuss:

Q *What do we want to tell [our buddy class] about the puzzle sticks?*

Remind the students that in order to make the puzzle, the directions need to be written in order. Ask:

Q *What is the first thing to do after taking apart the puzzle sticks? What should happen next? Then what?*

Q *What can [our buddy] do to check if the puzzle is solved correctly?*

Use the students' suggestions to write directions on a sheet of chart paper entitled, "Directions for Puzzle Sticks."

Directions for Puzzle Sticks

1. Take off the rubber band.

2. Lay out the sticks so the picture sides are all facing up.

3. Put the sticks together to make the picture.

4. Check the number on the back of each stick to see if you put it together correctly.

Collect the puzzle sticks and tell the students that you will deliver them, along with the directions, to the younger class.

SHARING AND REFLECTING

 Discuss Working Together

Ask and briefly discuss:

Q *What was [fun/challenging] about making the puzzles and trying them out?*

Q *What did you do to handle your partner's puzzle responsibly today? Why was that important to do?*

Explain that tomorrow the students will continue to explore functional writing.

Day 3

Materials

- "Writing Good Directions" chart
- Chart paper and a marker
- Loose, lined paper for each student

Selecting Topics

In this lesson, the students:

- Help write directions for how to do something
- Select a topic and begin drafting directions
- Explore sequence and completeness in functional writing
- Reach agreement before making decisions
- Share the work fairly

GETTING READY TO WRITE

 Briefly Review Functional Writing

Gather the class with partners sitting together, facing you. Have them bring their writing notebooks with them. Remind them that they have explored functional writing that tells how to take care of something and how to do something. Have the students open to the writing ideas section in their writing notebooks and review their lists of "Things I Take Care Of" and "Things I Know How to Do." Ask:

Q *What are some of the ideas you've listed under "Things I Take Care Of" and "Things I Know How to Do"?*

Explain that today the students will select something they know how to do and they will spend the next few days writing directions for that activity. They will eventually publish their directions as part of a class book for students to read and enjoy during independent reading time.

 Shared Writing: Directions for How to Do Something

Ask the students to watch as you model what they will do in the coming days. Name an everyday activity that most people know how to do (for example, brushing your teeth). Think aloud about who might read the directions for that activity and what you might include so the directions are complete (for example, materials needed, how to start and finish). Ask:

Q *What might I need to do this activity?*

Use the students' suggestions to write items needed for the activity on a sheet of chart paper. Then ask:

 Q *What do you do to brush your teeth? Turn to your partner.*

After a moment, signal for the students' attention and ask:

Q *What do you do first to [brush your teeth]? What do you do next?*

Use the students' suggestions to write the directions on the chart.

Brushing Your Teeth

<u>You Need:</u>

    Toothbrush
    Tube of toothpaste
    Mirror (optional)
    Sink and water

<u>Directions:</u>

1. Put a blob of toothpaste on your toothbrush.
2. Wet the brush.
3. Clench your teeth. Put the toothbrush in each cheek and brush up and down all along the outsides of your teeth.
4. Open your jaw and brush the insides of your top teeth and then your bottom teeth. Hold the toothbrush straight up and down to brush the insides of your front teeth.
5. Brush back and forth on the chewing surfaces.
6. Spit and then rinse your mouth.
7. Rinse your toothbrush and put it and the toothpaste away.

Reread the directions aloud and then ask:

Q *Does the order of the directions make sense? Why or why not?*

Q *Does the reader have all the directions needed to do the activity? Why or why not?*

Refer to the "Writing Good Directions" chart and remind the students that these are questions they should ask themselves when doing functional writing.

▶ ### 3 Get Ready to Write Directions

Explain that today partners will discuss and agree on something they both know how to do. After discussing how to do the activity and agreeing on the steps, each partner will write her own directions for the activity. They may pick something listed on their "Things I Take Care Of" and "Things I Know How to Do" lists, or they may pick something else. Ask and briefly discuss:

Q *What other everyday activities like [brushing your teeth] might you and your partner want to write about?*

Q *What can you and your partner do if you don't agree at first on an activity?*

Students might say:

"We can keep talking until we agree."

"We can make a list of things we both know how to do and pick something off that list."

Give partners a few minutes to discuss and agree on an activity.

WRITING TIME

▶ ### 4 Write Activity Directions

Distribute writing paper and remind the students to write on every other line. Have them return to their seats and work for 20–30 minutes on writing directions for their activity. Remind them to use your modeled activity directions to help them write their directions.

When the pairs seem to be working independently, begin conferring with one pair at a time.

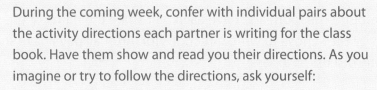

TEACHER CONFERENCE NOTE

During the coming week, confer with individual pairs about the activity directions each partner is writing for the class book. Have them show and read you their directions. As you imagine or try to follow the directions, ask yourself:

- Are the directions clear and easy to follow?

- Are the directions in an order that makes sense?

- Are the directions complete and accurate?

Support the students by asking questions such as:

Q *What do you need in order to do to this activity? How will you write that?*

Q *What is the first thing you do when you do this activity?*

Q *I'm confused by this direction. How can you rewrite the direction so it's clear?*

Q *What do you need to do to finish this activity? How will you write that?*

If partners have picked an activity that you feel is too complex for this writing assignment, help them pick a simpler activity to write about.

Document your observations for each pair using the "Conference Notes" record sheet (BLM1).

Signal to let the students know when writing time is over.

SHARING AND REFLECTING

 Share Topics

Briefly discuss:

Q *What was fun about writing your directions today? What was challenging?*

Go around the room and have each pair share the name of the activity they chose to write directions for. After all pairs have shared, briefly discuss as a class:

Q *What activity did you hear that you might like to learn how to do? Why?*

Explain that tomorrow partners will continue to work on their drafts.

Teacher Note

Save your charted model directions to use on Day 4 and throughout the unit.

Day 4

Drafting and Revising

In this lesson, the students:

- Explore accuracy and clarity in functional writing
- Continue to draft directions
- Reread and revise their directions
- Reach agreement before making decisions
- Share the work fairly

Materials

- Transparency of "Putting on Your Shoes and Socks" (BLM28)
- Your charted model directions from Day 3
- "Writing Good Directions" chart
- Loose, lined paper for each student
- *Assessment Resource Book*

GETTING READY TO WRITE

 1 **Explore Accuracy and Clarity in Game Directions**

Have partners get their notebooks and sit together at desks today. Remind the students that yesterday partners chose something they know how to do and began writing directions for a class book. Review the items on the "Writing Good Directions" chart and remind the students that they should be asking themselves these questions as they write their directions.

Show the transparency of "Putting on Your Shoes and Socks" and explain that this is a set of directions for an everyday activity. Read the directions aloud; then ask:

 Q *What do you notice about the directions for this activity? Turn to your partner.*

Signal for attention and have a few volunteers share their thinking with the class.

> **Students might say:**
>
> "The directions are out of order. I'm confused."
>
> "I agree with [Michael]. It tells about putting on your right sock but not your left."
>
> "In addition to what [Gala] said, 'Make the right shoe tight' is unclear."

Teacher Note   ▶

A more complete set of directions
might read:

1. Put on your right sock.

2. Put on your right shoe and tie
   the laces.

3. Put on your left sock.

4. Put on your left shoe and tie
   the laces.

5. Make sure both shoes are
   on tight.

You might point out that there
could be more than one correct
order for these directions. (For
example, the left sock and shoe
can go on before the right.)

Point out that, in addition to making sure things are in the right
order, authors of functional writing must be sure that their writing
is clear and accurate so their readers will not be confused. On the
"Writing Good Directions" chart, add *Are the directions accurate and
clear?* Explain that when directions are accurate and clear, the reader
knows exactly what to do. Ask:

Q   *What might be a more complete and accurate set of directions for
putting on your shoes and socks?*

Use the students' suggestions to write a more complete and
accurate set of directions on a sheet of chart paper.

Explain that today partners will continue to work on the activity
directions they started yesterday.

WRITING TIME

2▶ Work on Activity Directions

Write the following directions on the board and have partners work
on them for 20–30 minutes.

- Finish drafting your directions.

- Reread your directions and ask yourself the questions on the
  "Writing Good Directions" chart.

- Revise your directions, if needed.

If necessary, stop the class halfway through the writing time and
have the students ask themselves the questions on the "Writing
Good Directions" chart.

When the pairs seem to be working independently, walk around
and observe.

CLASS ASSESSMENT NOTE

Observe partners working and ask yourself:

- Are partners working together in a productive way?

- Are they sharing the work fairly?

- Are they writing directions that are clear and easy to follow?

- Are the directions complete and in an order that makes sense?

Support struggling pairs by asking questions such as:

Q *What do you need in order to do to this activity? How will you write that?*

Q *What is the first thing you do when you do this activity?*

Q *I'm confused by this direction. How can you rewrite the direction so it's clear?*

Q *What do you need to do to finish this activity? How will you write that?*

Record your observations in the *Assessment Resource Book*.

Signal to let the students know when writing time is over.

SHARING AND REFLECTING

 Discuss Partner Work

Ask and briefly discuss:

Q *What did you and your partner do to share the work fairly today? What do you want to do [the same way/differently] next time to share the work fairly?*

Explain that next week each pair will exchange their directions with another pair. Pairs will give each other feedback about their directions before publishing them.

GENRE: FUNCTIONAL WRITING

Writing Focus

- Students review directions for sequence, completeness, accuracy, and clarity.

- Students proofread their drafts for spelling, punctuation, and grammar.

- Students write a final version of their directions.

- Students present their directions to the class from the Author's Chair.

Social Focus

- Students make decisions and solve problems respectfully.

- Students act in fair and caring ways.

- Students help one another improve their writing.

DO AHEAD

- (Optional) If computers are available, consider having partners type and print their functional writing pieces for the book. Consider recruiting parent volunteers to help them do so.

TEACHER AS WRITER

"You never know what you will learn until you start writing."
— Anita Brookner

Think of something you know how to do well and imagine teaching someone else how to do it. Write a draft of the directions for this activity and then ask yourself the questions on the "Writing Good Directions" chart. Revise the draft, if needed. Consider giving the directions to a friend or colleague to try the activity and give you feedback.

Day 1

Materials

- "Writing Good Directions" chart
- *Assessment Resource Book*

Group Conferring and Revising

In this lesson, the students:

- Confer with another pair about their directions
- Explore sequence, completeness, accuracy, and clarity in functional writing
- Ask for and receive feedback about their writing
- Give feedback in a helpful way
- Revise their directions

GETTING READY TO WRITE

 Note

Consider combining pairs in such a way that English Language Learners who speak the same native language are in groups together. This will provide support for their discussion about the activities.

1▶ Exchange Directions and Play

Have partners get their activity directions from last week and sit together at desks today. Review that last week partners worked together to write directions for a class book. Explain that today pairs will form groups of four, then they will exchange directions with the other pair in the group, imagine following the other pair's directions to do the activity, and give helpful feedback. Tell the students that, as they try to follow the directions, you would like them to ask themselves the questions on the "Writing Good Directions" chart and be ready to give the other pair feedback about the questions. If necessary, review the questions on the chart.

Have pairs exchange directions and have them read and imagine following the directions.

2▶ Confer in Groups About Directions

After pairs have had sufficient time to read and try each other's directions, signal for the students' attention. Redirect their attention to the "Writing Good Directions" chart and have partners use "Think, Pair, Share" to first think about and then discuss each question on the chart:

Q *Does the order of the directions make sense?* [pause] *Turn to your partner.*

 Q *Does the reader have all of the information needed?* [pause] *Turn to your partner.*

 Q *Are the directions accurate and clear?* [pause] *Turn to your partner.*

After partners have discussed all three questions, explain that they will give feedback to the other pair in the group about the directions. Ask and briefly discuss:

Q *If you and your partner were confused about any of the directions, how might you give that feedback in a respectful and helpful way?*

> **Students might say:**
>
> "We could say, 'We're not sure we understand what this direction means. Could you please explain it?'"
>
> "We could say that we're not sure what to do first and what to do next, and we could talk about it."
>
> "We could say that we need more information to know what to do and ask what else they could say."
>
> "We could say that it would help to see a picture of a step and ask them to draw one."

Have pairs give each other feedback. As they confer, circulate and observe.

CLASS ASSESSMENT NOTE

Observe the students and ask yourself:

- Do the students give each other useful feedback?
- Do they give and receive the feedback respectfully?
- Do the students discuss possible revisions?

Note any difficulties you observe groups having in order to discuss as a class.

Record your observations in the *Assessment Resource Book*.

After most of the groups are finished talking, signal for attention. Ask and briefly discuss:

Q   *What feedback did you get that helped you?*

Q   *What was helpful about how the other pair talked to you? Take a moment to thank them.*

Q   *What suggestions do you have for how the other pair might give feedback in the future? Take a moment to tell them.*

Explain that during writing time today, pairs will use the feedback they received to help them revise their directions. Tell them that they will proofread their directions tomorrow and publish them for the class book later in the week.

WRITING TIME

 Revise and Complete Drafts

Have partners return to their seats and work on revising their directions for 20–30 minutes. If they finish, they may write whatever they choose for the rest of the period.

When the pairs seem to be working independently, confer with one pair at a time.

TEACHER CONFERENCE NOTE

This week continue to confer with individual pairs about the activity directions they are writing for the class book. Have them show and read you their directions. As you follow the directions (or imagine following them), ask yourself:

- Are the directions clear and easy to follow?
- Are the directions in an order that makes sense?
- Are the directions complete and accurate?

continues

TEACHER CONFERENCE NOTE *continued*

Support the students by asking questions such as:

Q *What do you need in order to do to this activity? How will you write that?*

Q *What is the first thing you do when you do this activity?*

Q *I'm confused by this direction. How can you rewrite the direction so it's clear?*

Q *What do you need to do to finish this activity? How will you write that?*

If partners have picked an activity that you feel is too complex for this writing assignment, help them pick a simpler activity to write about.

Document your observations for each pair using the "Conference Notes" record sheet (BLM1).

Signal to let the students know when writing time is over.

SHARING AND REFLECTING

 Reflect on Revisions

Ask and briefly discuss:

Q *What is one of the changes you and your partner made to your directions today? Read it to us. Why did you make this change?*

Explain that tomorrow partners will proofread their drafts and write final versions.

Day 2

Materials

- *Student Writing Handbooks*, word bank and proofreading notes section
- Supply of lined paper for final versions
- (Optional) Computers for word processing (See "Do Ahead" page 533)

Proofreading

In this lesson, the students:

- Proofread their drafts for spelling, punctuation, and grammar
- Write the final version of their piece
- Reach agreement before making decisions
- Share materials fairly

GETTING READY TO WRITE

 Discuss Proofreading for Spelling and Conventions

Have partners get their draft activity directions and *Student Writing Handbooks* and sit together at desks today. Remind the students that yesterday they revised their directions after receiving feedback from another pair and that their directions will ultimately go into a class book of directions for things they know how to do.

Teacher Note ▶

To provide your students with more practice using skills and conventions of written English, do the appropriate activities in the *Skill Practice Teaching Guide* with them.

Explain that today partners will work together to proofread their drafts and then start writing their final version. Remind them that they should use their word bank and proofreading notes to help them proofread their drafts for spelling and correctness. (These components were introduced in Unit 2, Week 3, Days 1 and 2 on pages 156–163.) Briefly review these procedures by reminding partners to:

- Circle words in their draft that they are unsure how to spell and look them up in their word bank. They will add any words that are not already in their word bank after looking up their correct spelling in a dictionary or other source.

- Use their proofreading notes as a list of things to check in their draft before publishing. They will correct any errors by crossing out the error on their draft and writing the correction next to it.

Ask and briefly discuss:

Q *How will you and your partner be sure you agree that something needs to be changed and how to change it?*

Q *What will you do if you don't agree at first?*

Encourage partners to keep their ideas in mind as they work together today.

WRITING TIME

 Proofread Drafts and Write Final Versions

Have partners work on proofreading their drafts. Provide lined paper to pairs who finish proofreading and are ready to begin their final versions. As they work, circulate, observe, and offer assistance. When the pairs seem to be working independently, confer with one pair at a time.

TEACHER CONFERENCE NOTE

Continue to confer with individual pairs about the activity directions they are writing for the class book. Have them show and read you their directions. As you follow the directions (or imagine following them), ask yourself:

- Are the directions clear and easy to follow?
- Are the directions in an order that makes sense?
- Are the directions complete and accurate?

Support the students by asking questions such as:

Q *What do you need in order to do to this activity? How will you write that?*

Q *What is the first thing you do when you do this activity?*

Q *I'm confused by this direction. How can you rewrite the direction so it's clear?*

continues

> **TEACHER CONFERENCE NOTE** *continued*
>
> **Q** *What do you need to do to finish this activity? How will you write that?*
>
> If partners have picked an activity that you feel is too complex for this writing activity, help them pick a simpler activity to write about.
>
> Document your observations for each pair using the "Conference Notes" record sheet (BLM1).

Signal to let the students know when writing time is over.

SHARING AND REFLECTING

▶3 **Reflect on Proofreading**

Ask and briefly discuss:

Q *What words did you find in your word bank today? How did you check on words that were not in the word bank?*

Q *What corrections did you make in your draft after reviewing your proofreading notes?*

Explain that partners will finish working on their final versions tomorrow.

Day 3

Publishing

In this lesson, the students:

- Finish writing their final version
- Present their activity directions from the Author's Chair
- Express interest in and appreciation for one another's writing
- Ask one another questions about their writing

Materials

- Supply of lined paper for final versions
- Two chairs to use for Author's Chair sharing

GETTING READY TO WRITE

1 ▶ Briefly Review

Have partners sit together at desks today. Explain that they will finish working on the final versions of their activity directions. Pairs who finish will begin sharing their pieces from the Author's Chair after the writing time.

Write the following tasks on the board and read them aloud:

- Finish proofreading your draft using your word bank and proofreading notes.

- Finish writing the final version of your directions.

Have the students think quietly to themselves for a moment about the following question:

Q *What do you need to work on today to be ready to share your activity directions from the Author's Chair?*

After a moment, have the students begin working independently.

WRITING TIME

2 ▶ Finish Final Versions

Have partners work on their final versions. If they finish, they may write about anything they choose. As they work, circulate, observe, and offer assistance. When the pairs seem to be working independently, confer with one pair at a time.

TEACHER CONFERENCE NOTE

Continue to confer with individual pairs about the activity directions they are writing for the class book. Have them show and read you their directions. As you follow the directions (or imagine following them), ask yourself:

- Are the directions clear and easy to follow?

- Are the directions in an order that makes sense?

- Are the directions complete and accurate?

Support the students by asking questions such as:

Q *What do you need in order to do to this activity? How will you write that?*

Q *What is the first thing you do when you do this activity?*

Q *I'm confused by this direction. How can you rewrite the direction so it's clear?*

Q *What do you need to do to finish this activity? How will you write that?*

If partners have picked an activity that you feel is too complex for this writing assignment, help them pick a simpler activity to write about.

Document your observations for each pair using the "Conference Notes" record sheet (BLM1).

Signal to let the students know when writing time is over.

SHARING AND REFLECTING

 Conduct Author's Chair Sharing

Gather the class with partners sitting together, facing the Authors' Chairs. Remind authors to speak in a loud, clear voice and remind the audience to show interest in and appreciation for their classmates' writing.

Call on a pair to come to the Authors' Chairs and read their activity directions aloud. As they read, have the rest of the students close their eyes and imagine doing the activity.

At the end of the sharing, facilitate a discussion using questions like those that follow, and give the authors an opportunity to respond to the class's comments and questions.

Q *What did you learn about [making paper airplanes] from this pair's directions?*

Q *What questions can we ask [Gwen] and [Joanne] about what they wrote?*

Follow this procedure to have other pairs share from the Authors' Chairs.

 Reflect on Audience Behavior During Author's Chair Sharing

Ask and briefly discuss:

Q *What did we do well as an audience today? What do we still want to work on the next time our authors share their work?*

Q *If you shared today, how did the audience make you feel? What did they do that made you feel [relaxed/nervous/proud]?*

Explain that more pairs will share their directions from the Authors' Chairs tomorrow.

Teacher Note

As pairs share their directions from the Authors' Chairs, collect them to compile into two identical books for the class library.

Day 4

Materials

- Supply of lined paper for final versions
- "Writing Good Directions" chart
- Two chairs to use for Author's Chair sharing

Publishing

In this lesson, the students:

- Reflect on functional writing
- Finish writing their final versions
- Present their activity directions from the Author's Chair
- Express interest in and appreciation for one another's writing
- Ask one another questions about their writing

GETTING READY TO WRITE

FACILITATION TIP

Reflect on your experience over the past three weeks with **avoiding repeating or paraphrasing** students' responses. Does this practice feel natural to you? Are you integrating it into class discussions throughout the school day? What effect is it having on the students? Are they participating more responsibly in class discussions? We encourage you to continue to try this practice and reflect on students' responses as you facilitate class discussions in the future. (See the front matter for special considerations for English Language Learners.)

▶1 Review and Reflect on Functional Writing

Have partners sit together at desks today. Remind them that they have been exploring functional writing that gives directions for how to do something. Direct their attention to the "Writing Good Directions" chart and review the items on the chart aloud. In pairs and as a class, discuss:

 Q *Which of these questions were the most challenging for you to think about as you wrote your directions, and why? Turn to your partner.*

Q *What did you like best about writing your directions?*

Q *What have you learned about functional writing?*

Remind the students that writers become better over time as they practice writing over and over. Encourage the students who feel drawn to functional writing to continue to read and write it during their free time and during the open weeks of this program.

Explain that today partners will finish writing the final version of their directions and share them from the Authors' Chairs.

WRITING TIME

 Finish Final Versions

Have partners work on their final versions. If they have already finished, they may write anything else they choose.

As the students work, circulate, observe, and offer assistance. When pairs seem to be working independently, confer with one pair at a time.

TEACHER CONFERENCE NOTE

Continue to confer with individual pairs about the activity directions they are writing for the class book. Have them show and read you their directions. As you follow the directions (or imagine following them), ask yourself:

* Are the directions clear and easy to follow?

* Are the directions in an order that makes sense?

* Are the directions complete and accurate?

Support the students by asking questions such as:

Q *What do you need in order to do to this activity? How will you write that?*

Q *What is the first thing you do when you do this activity?*

Q *I'm confused by this direction. How can you rewrite the direction so it's clear?*

Q *What do you need to do to finish this activity? How will you write that?*

Document your observations for each pair using the "Conference Notes" record sheet (BLM1).

Signal to let the students know when writing time is over.

SHARING AND REFLECTING

▶3 Conduct Author's Chair Sharing

Gather the class with partners sitting together, facing the Authors' Chairs. As you did yesterday, remind authors to speak in a loud, clear voice. Also remind the audience to show interest in and appreciation for their classmates' writing.

Call on a pair to come to the Authors' Chairs and read their directions aloud. At the end of the sharing, facilitate a discussion using questions like those that follow, and give the authors an opportunity to respond to the class's comments and questions.

Q *What did you learn about [riding a bicycle] from this pair's directions?*

Q *What questions can we ask [Pedro] and [Kaitlin] about what they wrote?*

Follow this procedure to have other pairs share from the Authors' Chairs.

▶4 Reflect on Audience Behavior During Author's Chair Sharing

Ask and briefly discuss:

Q *What did we do well as an audience today? What do we still want to work on the next time authors share their work?*

Q *If you shared today, how did the audience make you feel? What did they do that made you feel [relaxed/nervous/proud]?*

Assure pairs that haven't yet shared that they will get to share their piece from the Authors' Chairs in the coming days. Explain that after all of the directions are read aloud, you will compile them into two identical books (one book for each partner's directions) and place the books in the class library so the students can read and enjoy them on their own.

Teacher Note

If necessary, repeat today's lesson for a few more days, or even another week, to give all the pairs time to finish their directions. Students who finish may begin a new piece of writing (functional writing or otherwise) or continue working on a piece of writing they started earlier.

Even if you decide to begin another genre unit immediately, continue to have pairs share their activity directions from the Authors' Chairs until everyone has had a chance to do so.

Teacher Note

This is the last week of the unit. You will need to reassign partners before beginning the next unit.

EXTENSION

Write Letters Home About Functional Writing

Provide letter-writing practice for the students by having them write a letter home about what they learned about functional writing. Stimulate their thinking by reviewing the "Giving Good Directions" chart and discussing questions such as:

Q *What did you learn about functional writing?*

Q *What steps did you go through to develop and publish your directions?*

Q *What functional writing might you read or write at home?*

If necessary, review the elements of a letter (date, salutation, body, closing, and signature) by modeling or writing a shared sample letter with the class. Have the students write and proofread their letters; then attach each student's letter to a copy of his published activity directions and send it home.

Revisiting the Writing Community

Revisiting the Writing Community

Unit 7

Revisiting the Writing Community

During this one-week unit, the students review the writing they have done this year and reflect on their growth as writers and as members of the classroom writing community. They plan their summer writing and write letters to next year's class about what it means to be a writer. They thank their classmates for supporting them this year, and they express interest in and appreciation for one another's writing and thinking.

UNIT OVERVIEW

WEEK	DAY 1	DAY 2	DAY 3	DAY 4
1	**Reflecting on Writing** **Focus:** Reflect on growth as writers	**Reflecting on Writing** **Focus:** Write to next year's class about how to be a good writer	**Planning for Writing** **Focus:** Plan summer writing	**Reflecting on Community** **Focus:** Reflect on growth as community members; thank classmates

Week 1 Overview

UNIT 7: REVISITING THE WRITING COMMUNITY

Writing Focus

- Students review their writing from the year.

- Student reflect on their growth as writers.

- Students write to next year's class about how to be a good writer.

- Students plan their summer writing.

Social Focus

- Students build the writing community.

- Students act in fair and caring ways.

- Students build on one another's thinking.

- Students express interest in and appreciation for one another's writing.

DO AHEAD

- Prior to Day 1, gather all the students' published writing from the classroom library, including individual pieces, pair work, and class books. Return each student's work to him or her, disassembling class books. You might copy pair work and have partners decide who will take the original and who will take the copy. If necessary, provide folders so the students can keep all of their pieces together.

Day 1

Materials

- Students' published writing, returned to them (see "Do Ahead" on page 551)
- Pad of small, self-stick notes for each student
- "Conference Notes" record sheet for each student (BLM1)
- *Assessment Resource Book*

Reflecting on Writing

In this lesson, the students:

- Review their writing from the year
- Reflect and write about how they have grown as writers
- Think about challenges they faced and what they have learned about writing
- Listen to the thinking of others and share their own
- Express interest in and appreciation for one another's writing

GETTING READY TO WRITE

Teacher Note

You will not assign new partners for this week. Either have the students work with their partner from the previous unit or simply have them turn and talk to someone sitting near them during "Turn to Your Partner."

Teacher Note

This lesson may require an extended class period.

1 ▶ Discuss Goals for the Week

Have the students stay at their desks for the lesson today. Have them get their writing notebooks, published writing from the year, and a pencil.

Explain that during this last week of the *Being a Writer* program, the students will review the writing they did this year, think about how they have changed and grown as writers and as members of a writing community, reflect and write about what they have learned about good writing, and plan their summer writing.

2 ▶ Review Published Writing from the Year

Distribute a pad of self-stick notes to each student and explain that they will first look through their published pieces from the year. Write the following questions on the board and tell the students that you would like them to think about the questions as they review their pieces.

> - What is one of the best published pieces of writing you
>   have done this year? Mark it with the word "Best" on a
>   self-stick note.
>
> - What piece of writing did you have the most fun
>   working on this year? Mark it with the word "Fun" on
>   a self-stick note.
>
> - What piece of writing was the most challenging for you?
>   Mark it with the word "Challenging" on a self-stick note.

Point out that the students might decide to put multiple self-stick notes on a single piece of writing.

Give the students ample time to look through their published pieces and mark them with self-stick notes. When most students have marked their best, most fun, and most challenging pieces, signal for their attention. Have them separate out the marked pieces of writing and put their other published pieces away.

 ## Review Notebook Writing

Explain that for each of the flagged pieces, the students will find the drafts they wrote for those pieces in their notebooks and mark them with self-stick notes. Tell them you would like them to reread those drafts and try to remember what was it was like to write them.

Give the students ample time to review their notebooks. Then signal for their attention.

 ## Share Marked Pieces with Another Student

Explain that the students will share their thinking about the three pieces of writing they marked with another student sitting near them. Encourage them to tell each other what they remember about working on each piece and why they chose those three as their best, most fun, and most challenging.

As partners share, walk around, listen, and observe.

CLASS ASSESSMENT NOTE

Listen to students as they share in pairs and ask yourself:

* Are the students able to explain why they marked a piece as their best, most fun, or most challenging?

* Do they refer to their first drafts or other steps in the writing process in talking about their pieces?

* Do they listen carefully to each other?

Record your observations in the *Assessment Resource Book*.

After allowing enough time for both partners to share their writing, signal for attention. Have a few volunteers share with the class about one piece of writing they marked and what they thought about it.

5▶ Get Ready to Write About Growth as Writers

Ask the students to look at the first couple of drafts they wrote in their notebooks and to compare them to the last few drafts they wrote. After a moment, ask the students to think quietly to themselves as they listen to the following questions. Ask the questions one at a time, pausing between each question to give the students time to think.

Q *What do you notice about the way you wrote at the beginning of the year, compared to the way you write now?*

Q *What kinds of words did you use in your early pieces, compared to your more recent pieces?*

Q *How do you think you have changed as a writer this year?*

Without sharing as a class, explain that you would like the students to open to the next blank page in their notebooks and write their reflections about how they think they have grown or changed as a writer this year, based on looking at their work from the beginning and end of the year. They do not need to write answers for each question you asked.

WRITING TIME

6 ▶ Write Reflections About Growth as Writers

Have the students write their reflections silently for 10–20 minutes. If they finish, they may write about anything they choose.

> **TEACHER CONFERENCE NOTE**
>
> You may wish to confer once more with individual students this week, using their three marked pieces of writing as the topic of the conference. Have each student show you the pieces she flagged as her best, most fun, and most challenging and tell you what she remembers about working on those pieces and why she flagged them as such.
>
> Document your observations for each student using the "Conferent Notes" record sheet (BLM1). Use the "Conference Notes" record sheets during conferences throughout this week.

Signal to let the students know when writing time is over.

SHARING AND REFLECTING

7 ▶ Share Reflections

Ask the students to reread what they wrote today and underline a sentence that tells one way they think they have grown or changed as a writer this year. Give them a moment to select their sentence, and then go around the room and have each student read his sentence aloud to the class, without comment.

When all the students have read their sentence about how they have grown or changed, ask and briefly discuss as a class:

Q *What did you hear about how your classmates have grown as writers this year?*

Q *What questions do you want to ask a classmate about the sentence he or she shared?*

Explain that tomorrow the students will continue to reflect on how they have grown and what they have learned as writers.

Day 2

Reflecting on Writing

In this lesson, the students:

- Write to next year's class about ways to be a good writer
- Get ideas by listening to others

GETTING READY TO WRITE

1 **Review Genres Explored This Year**

Have the students stay at their desks today. Remind them that they reflected yesterday on how they have changed or grown as writers over the past year. Point out that they have learned a lot about how to be good writers of personal narratives, fiction stories, nonfiction informational pieces, functional writing, and poetry.

Explain that today the students will reflect on what they have learned about how to be a good writer. Then they will write letters to next year's third grade class to help them become good writers.

2 **Reflect on Ways to Be a Good Writer**

Use "Think, Pair, Share" to have the students first think about and then discuss:

Q *What have you learned about how to be a good writer?* [pause] *Turn to your partner.*

After the students have talked in pairs, signal for their attention and have volunteers report their thinking to the class. As they share, record their ideas on a sheet of chart paper entitled, "Ways to Be a Good Writer."

Materials

- *Student Writing Handbooks*
- Chart paper and a marker
- Loose, lined paper for writing letters
- *Assessment Resource Book*

◀ **Teacher Note**

If the students have difficulty generating ideas for this question, suggest some ideas like those in the "Students might say" note; then ask, "What else have you learned about how to be a good writer?"

Students might say:

"I learned that good writers often use sensory details to help the reader imagine what's happening."

"I learned that to be a good writer you have to make sure your writing makes sense to people."

"To be a good writer, you have to be able to think about things and revise your writing so it gets better."

"I learned that writers become good because they practice writing all the time."

"I learned that good writers write what they are interested in."

Ways to Be a Good Writer

- Use sensory details.
- Check to see if it makes sense.
- Revise to improve your writing.
- Practice writing all the time.
- Write about what interests you.

Explain that during writing time today, the students will each write a letter to next year's third grade class, giving them some advice to help them become good writers. Tell them that they may include things listed on the chart as well as other ideas they have. Point out that the letters should be written in their own words and should be friendly and encouraging in tone.

If necessary, write the date and a salutation (for example, "Dear Next Year's Third Graders") where everyone can see it so the students can copy these if they need to. Also remind them to sign their name at the bottom of their letters when they finish.

WRITING TIME

 Independently Write Letters to Next Year's Class

Distribute loose, lined paper and have the students write their letters for 20–30 minutes. If they finish, have them proofread their letters for spelling and punctuation using the word bank and proofreading notes sections of their *Student Writing Handbooks*.

As the students work, walk around the room and observe them.

CLASS ASSESSMENT NOTE

Observe the students and ask yourself:

- Do the students write confidently about ways to be a good writer?

- Do students who seemed cautious or inhibited about their writing early in the year write more freely now?

- Do they confidently use the word bank and proofreading notes to proofread their writing?

Record your observations in the *Assessment Resource Book*.

Signal to let the students know when writing time is over.

SHARING AND REFLECTING

4 Share Letters and Reflect on Work Together

Have the students share their letters with someone sitting next to them. Remind them to listen carefully to their partner's letter so they can share what their partner wrote with the class.

After giving students time to share, signal for their attention and discuss:

Q *What advice did your partner include in his letter to next year's class?*

Q *Is your partner's letter friendly and encouraging? What does she write to make it feel that way?*

Q *What did you do to help your work with your partner go well today?*

Teacher Note

If necessary, give the students time to finish writing and proofreading their letters, then collect them into a binder to share with your incoming class this fall.

Day 3

Materials

- "Writing Habits of Professional Authors" (see page 566)
- A highlighter or marker for each student

Planning for Writing

In this lesson, the students:

- Learn about the writing habits of professional authors
- Plan their summer writing
- Get ideas by listening to others
- Express interest in and appreciation for one another's writing

GETTING READY TO WRITE

1 ### Generate Topics to Write About Over the Summer

Have the students stay at their desks today. Review that they have been looking back over the year and thinking about what they have learned and how they have grown as writers. Tell them that today they will look forward and think about how they plan to keep writing over the summer.

Ask the students to open to the writing ideas section of their writing notebooks and to review the ideas they wrote over the year. After sufficient time for the students to review their ideas, ask:

 Q *What are some ideas you didn't get a chance to write about this year that you are still interested in writing about? Turn and talk to someone sitting next to you.*

Distribute a highlighter or marker to each student and explain that you would like them to highlight or mark ideas in their notebooks that they are still interested in writing about. After they have had a chance to highlight their ideas, ask them to turn to a clean page and spend a few more minutes brainstorming and listing other ideas they might want to write about this summer. After a moment, ask and discuss as a class:

Q   *What are some things you might want to write about this summer?*

Q   *Why is it important for you to keep writing on your own this summer?*

> **Students might say:**
>
> "It's important to keep writing on our own so we don't forget how to be good writers over the summer."
>
> "It's important to keep writing so we can keep getting better at writing."
>
> "In addition to what [Ansel] said, it's important to keep writing because it's fun!"

Point out that most professional authors have daily habits that help them keep writing. They have a special time and place in which they write, and they write for a certain length of time. Sometimes they use particular materials, like a certain pen or kind of paper. Explain that today you will read some quotes by professional authors about their writing habits. The students will then think about what kinds of habits they want to have to help them keep writing over the summer.

▶2 Read and Discuss Some Professional Authors' Writing Habits

Read "Writing Habits of Professional Authors" aloud slowly and clearly, clarifying vocabulary as you read.

> **Suggested Vocabulary**
>
> **cubicle:** a small work area
> **lull:** short, quiet break
> **teak:** a kind of wood

Ask and briefly discuss:

Q   *What habits did you hear about?*

Q   *What ideas did this give you about habits you can set for yourself at home to help you keep writing this summer?*

Explain that during writing time today, you would like the students to write in their notebooks about what they will do to help them continue to write this summer. Encourage them to write specific habits they want to establish, such as where, when, how often, and how long they will write each day. Also invite them to think about what objects they would like to have around them to help them write.

If the students finish, they may add to their list of topics to write about this summer or choose one of those ideas and write about it.

WRITING TIME

 ### Write Independently About Writing Habits

Write the following directions on the board and have the students work quietly for 20–30 minutes.

- Write about what you will do to help yourself continue writing this summer.

- Add to your list of topics to write about over the summer.

- Pick one of your summer topics and start writing about it.

As the students work, walk around and observe or continue to confer with individual students (see the Teacher Conference Note on Day 1, page 555).

Signal to let the students know when writing time is over.

SHARING AND REFLECTING

 ### Share Plans for Summer Writing

Ask the students to reread what they wrote today and underline a sentence that tells one thing they will do to help them keep writing this summer. Give them a moment to select their sentence, then go around the room and have each student read her sentence aloud to the class, without comment.

When all the students have read their sentence, ask and briefly discuss as a class:

Q *What ideas did you hear that you want to add to your list?*

Q *What questions do you want to ask a classmate about the sentence he or she shared?*

Give the students a moment to add ideas to their lists, if they wish. Encourage them to continue writing as much as they can this summer and to focus on enjoying their own writing.

Day 4

Reflecting on Community

In this lesson, the students:

- Reflect on their contributions to the writing community
- Reflect on how they have benefited from the writing community
- Thank one another for their help

GETTING READY TO SHARE

Making Meaning® Teacher

Some questions in this lesson are similar to those asked in *Making Meaning* Unit 8, Week 2, Days 3 and 4. Read the lessons in both programs and decide if you want to teach them separately or combine them into one experience for the students. It is not necessary to ask the same question in both lessons.

1 ▶ Reflect on Classroom Writing Community

Have the students stay at their desks today. Remind them that they reflected on how they have grown as writers earlier in the week. Explain that today they will have a chance to think about how they did with becoming a safe and caring writing community this year and how they have personally grown as members of the community.

Have the students close their eyes and visualize as you ask each of the following questions. Pause between each question to give them time to think.

Q *What has it felt like to be a part of our writing community this year?*

Q *What have you done to contribute to our community this year?*

Teacher Note

Some ways students have helped each other this year to become better writers include: brainstorming ideas together, giving each other feedback, working on some writing projects together (such as their nonfiction informational piece), asking each other questions about their writing, and showing interest and appreciation when sharing from the Author's Chair.

Q *What are three things your partners or classmates have done to help you to become a better writer this year?*

Have the students open their eyes, turn to the next blank page in their writing notebooks, and write the three things their classmates or partners have done to help them become better writers this year.

After the students have had time to list their ideas, signal for their attention.

SHARING AND REFLECTING

 Share Reflections and Thank One Another

Gather the class in a circle and have them bring their writing
notebooks. Explain that each student will choose one of the three
things they listed to read aloud to the class. Point out that it is
important to take time to thank people who have been helpful to
them, and invite them to say "Thank you" to the class after reading
their selection aloud.

Give the students a moment to select what they will read aloud,
then go around the room and have each student read his selection
aloud, followed by "Thank you." When all the students have read
their selections, ask and discuss:

Q *How have we done at creating a caring and safe community this
year? What makes you think so?*

Q *How have you grown in your ability to work with partners this year?*

Students might say:

"I think we did a good job becoming a community this year.
 Whenever we had problems, we talked about them so we could
 get along better."

"I agree with [Paulie] because the more we got to know each
 other, the more we were a community."

"I used to be too shy to talk to my partner, but now I feel I can
 talk to any partner I have."

You might want to share some of your general observations about
ways your students have changed or grown as members of the
community over the year.

Encourage the students to continue to write and to become caring
members of their classroom writing community next year.

◀ **Teacher Note**

You might say, "I remember how
some students didn't want to
work with their assigned partner
at the beginning of the year. Now
you are much better at working
with any partner. I also notice that
you relied much more heavily on
me at the beginning of the year
to help you solve your problems.
Now you are able to solve many
problems by yourself."

Excerpts

Writing Habits of Professional Authors

"Get up very early and get going at once; in fact [write] first and wash afterwards."

— W. H. Auden

"I generally write for three or four hours at a sitting, mornings as a rule."

— Saul Bellow

"The writer…withdraws to some quiet corner, a bedroom perhaps, or any cubicle with a chair and a table, and applies himself to his blank paper. Two hours a day are needed, three hours are better, four are heroic."

— Gerald Warner Brace

"My goal is to write only one sentence a day. I write this on the bus on my way to work. I usually find that I write more than just one sentence, but the important point is that I have accomplished the goal I set by 9:00 A.M."

— Lavinia Dobler

"I keep a typewriter with a sheet of paper in it on the end of the kitchen table. When I have a five-minute lull and the children are playing quietly, I sit down and knock out a paragraph."

— Lois Duncan

"I have a nice teak desk, long and wide, on which I keep special things: crisp new legal pads and No. 2 pencils with good rubber erasers that don't leave red smears; a dark blue draftsman lamp that twists and bends like a tall, limber skeleton; a small quartz clock that silently flicks the minutes…and an orange tomcat who lies on a blanket and snores."

— Gail Godwin

Appendices

Grade 3 Skill Development Chart

Grade 3 Skill Development Chart

X = skill taught/practiced

Skill/Convention code	Prewriting	Drafting	Revision	Proofreading	Publication	Capitalize proper nouns (including holidays and special events)	Use apostrophes to show possession	Use quotation marks to punctuate speech	Use commas in a series	Recognize and correct incomplete sentences	Correctly use commonly misused words	Capitalize the first letters of sentences and use punctuation at the ends	Recognize and use parts of speech
3.1.1	X	X											
3.1.2	X	X											
3.1.3	X	X											
3.1.4	X	X											
3.1.5	X	X											
3.1.6	X	X											
3.2.1			X										
3.2.2			X										X
3.2.3			X	X	X	X						X	
3.3.1	X	X											
3.3.2	X	X											
3.3.3			X										
3.3.4			X	X	X	X					X	X	
3.4.1	X	X											
3.4.2	X	X											
3.4.3	X	X											
3.4.4			X										
3.4.5			X										X
3.4.6			X	X	X	X		X		X	X	X	
3.5.1	X												
3.5.2	X												
3.5.3	X	X											
3.5.4		X											
3.5.5			X										
3.5.6			X	X	X	X		X		X	X	X	X
3.6.1	X	X											
3.6.2	X	X											
3.6.3			X	X	X			X		X		X	X
3.7.1	X	X			X								

Bibliography

Ainsworth, Mary. "Patterns of Attachment Behaviour Shown by the Infant in Interaction with His Mother." *Merrill-Palmer Quarterly* 10 (1964): 51–58.

Anderson, Richard C., and P. David Pearson. "A Schema-Theoretic View of Basic Process in Reading Comprehension." In *Handbook of Reading Research* edited by P. David Pearson. New York: Longman, 1984.

Asher, James J. "Children Learning Another Language: A Developmental Hypothesis." *Child Development* 48 (1977): 1040–48.

———. "Children's First Language as a Model for Second Language Learning." *Modern Language Journal* 56 (1972): 133–39.

———. "The Strategy of Total Physical Response: An Application to Learning Russian." *International Review of Applied Linguistics* 3 (1965): 291–300.

Atwell, Nancie. *In the Middle: New Understandings About Writing, Reading, and Learning*. Portsmouth, NH: Heinemann-Boynton/Cook, 1998.

Battistich, Victor, Daniel Solomon, Dong-il Kim, Marilyn Watson, and Eric Schaps. "Schools as Communities, Poverty Levels of Student Populations, and Students' Attitudes, Motives, and Performance: A Multilevel Analysis." *American Educational Research Journal* 32, no. 3 (Fall 1995): 627–58.

Beck, Isabel L., Margaret G. McKeown, and Linda Kucan. *Bringing Words to Life: Robust Vocabulary Instruction*. New York: Guilford Press, 2002.

Bowlby, John. *Attachment and Loss*. Vol 1, *Attachment*. New York: Basic Books, 1997.

Calkins, Lucy. *The Art of Teaching Writing*. Portsmouth, NH: Heinemann, 1994.

Contestable, Julie W., Shaila Regan, Susie Alldredge, Carol Westrich, and Laurel Robertson. *Number Power: A Cooperative Approach to Mathematics and Social Development Grades K–6*. Oakland, CA: Developmental Studies Center, 1999.

Culham, Ruth. *6+1 Traits of Writing: The Complete Guide for the Primary Grades*. Portland, OR: Northwest Regional Educational Laboratory, 2005.

———. *6+1 Traits of Writing: The Complete Guide, Grades 3 and Up*. Portland, OR: Northwest Regional Educational Laboratory, 2003.

Cummins, James. "The Role of Primary Language Development in Promoting Educational Success for Language Minority Students." In *Schooling and Language Minority Students: A Theoretical Framework*. Los Angeles: California State University, Evaluation, Dissemination, and Assessment Center, 1981.

Cunningham, Anne E., and Keith E. Stanovich. "What Reading Does for the Mind." *American Educator*, Spring/Summer 1998: 8–15.

Developmental Studies Center. *Blueprints for a Collaborative Classroom*. Oakland, CA: Developmental Studies Center, 1997.

———. *Ways We Want Our Class to Be*. Oakland, CA: Developmental Studies Center, 1996.

DeVries, Rheta, and Betty Zan. *Moral Classrooms, Moral Children*. New York: Teachers College Press, 1994.

Dewey, John. *Democracy and Education*. New York: Macmillan, 1916.

Fletcher, Ralph, and JoAnn Portalupi. *Writing Workshop: The Essential Guide*. Portsmouth, NH: Heinemann, 2001.

Flood, James, Dianne Lapp, and Julie M. Jensen. *The Handbook of Research on Teaching the English Language*. Mahwah, NJ: Lawrence Erlbaum Associates, 2002.

Freedman, Sarah W., Linda Flower, Glynda Hull, and J. R. Hayes. "Ten Years of Research: Achievements of the National Center for the Study of Writing and Literacy." In *A Handbook for Literacy Educators: Research on Teaching the Communicative and Visual Arts*, edited by J. Flood, S. B. Heath, and D. Lapp. Forthcoming.

Gambrell, Linda B., Lesley Mandel Morrow, Susan B. Neuman, and Michael Pressley, eds. *Best Practices in Literacy Instruction*. New York: Guilford Press, 1999.

Graves, Donald H. "Children Can Write Authentically If We Help Them." *Primary Voices K–6* 1, no. 1 (2003): 2–6.

Graves, Donald H. *Writing: Teachers and Children at Work*. Portsmouth, NH: Heinemann, 2003.

Hakuta, Kenji, Yuko Goto Butler, and Daria Witt. *How Long Does It Take English Learners to Attain Proficiency?* Santa Barbara, CA: University of California, Linguistic Minority Research Institute, 2000.

Harvey, Stephanie. *Nonfiction Matters: Reading, Writing, and Research in Grades 3–8*. York, ME: Stenhouse Publishers, 1998.

Herrell, Adrienne L. *Fifty Strategies for Teaching English Language Learners.* Upper Saddle River, NJ: Merrill, 2000.

Johnson, David W., Roger T. Johnson, and Edythe Johnson Holubec. *The New Circles of Learning: Cooperation in the Classroom.* Alexandria, VA: Association for Supervision and Curriculum Development, 1994.

Kagan, Spencer. *Cooperative Learning.* San Juan Capistrano, CA: Resources of Teachers, 1992.

Kamil, Michael L., Peter B. Mosenthal, P. David Pearson, and Rebecca Barr, eds. *Handbook of Reading Research, Volume III.* Mahwah, NJ: Lawrence Erlbaum Associates, 2000.

Kelley, Michael C. *Teachers' Reports of Writing Instruction at a High Performing Elementary School.* University of Delaware: Doctoral dissertation, 2002.

Kohlberg, Lawrence. *The Psychology of Moral Development.* New York: Harper and Row, 1984.

Kohn, Alfie. *Beyond Discipline: From Compliance to Community.* Alexandria, VA: Association for Supervision and Curriculum Development, 1996.

———. *Punished by Rewards: The Trouble with Gold Stars, Incentive Plans, A's, Praise, and Other Bribes.* New York: Houghton Mifflin Company, 1999.

Krashen, Stephen D. *Principles and Practice in Second Language Acquisition.* New York: Prentice-Hall, 1982.

———. *Second Language Acquisition and Second Language Learning.* New York: Pergamon Press, 1981.

———. "TPR: Still a Very Good Idea." *NovELTy* 5, no. 4 (1998).

———, and Tracy D. Terrell. *The Natural Approach: Language Acquisition in the Classroom.* Englewood Cliffs, NJ: Prentice Hall, 1983.

National Commission on Writing in America's Colleges and Schools. *The Neglected "R": The Need for a Writing Revolution.* New York: College Board, 2003.

National Council of Teachers of English. *What We Know About Writing: Early Literacy.* NCTE Writing Initiative. www.ncte.org/prog/writing/research/113328.htm.

National Governor's Association for Best Practices. *Making Writing Instruction Work.* Washington, DC: National Governor's Association Center for Best Practices, 2001.

Nucci, Larry P., ed. *Moral Development and Character Education: A Dialogue*. Berkeley, CA: McCutchan Publishing Corporation, 1989.

Optiz, Michael F., ed. *Literacy Instruction for Culturally and Linguistically Diverse Students*. Newark, DE: International Reading Association, 1998.

Piaget, Jean. *The Child's Conception of the World*. Trans. Joan and Andrew Tomlinson. Lanham, MD: Littlefield Adams, 1969.

———. *The Moral Judgment of the Child*. Trans. Marjorie Gabain. New York: The Free Press, 1965.

Ray, Katie Wood. *About the Authors: Writing Workshop with Our Youngest Writers*. Portsmouth, NH: Heinemann, 2004.

Resnick, Michael D., P. S. Bearman, R. W. Blum, K. E. Bauman, K. M. Harris, J. Jones, J. Tabor, et al. "Protecting Adolescents from Harm: Findings from the National Longitudinal Study on Adolescent Health." *Journal of the American Medical Association* 278 (1997): 823–32.

Schaps, Eric, Victor Battistich, and Dan Solomon. "Community in School a Key to Student Growth: Findings from the Child Development Project." In *Building School Success on Social and Emotional Learning*, edited by R. Weissberg, J. Zins, and H. Walbert. New York: Teachers College Press, 2004.

Schaps, Eric, Catherine Lewis, and Marilyn Watson. "Building Classroom Communities." *Thrust for Educational Leadership*, September 1997.

Schaps, Eric, Esther F. Schaeffer, and Sanford N. McDonnell. "What's Right and Wrong in Character Education Today." *Education Week*, September 12, 2001: 40–44.

Shefelbine, John, and Katherine K. Newman. *SIPPS: Systematic Instruction in Phoneme Awareness, Phonics, and Sight Words*. Oakland, CA: Developmental Studies Center, 2005.

Sulzby, Elizabeth. "Research Directions: Transitions from Emergent to Conventional Writing." *Language Arts* 69 (1992): 290–97.

Swain, M., and S. Lapkin. "Problems in Output and the Cognitive Processes They Generate: A Step Toward Second Language Learning." *Applied Linguistics* 16, no. 3 (1995): 371–91.

William, Joan A. "Classroom Conversations: Opportunities to Learn for ESL Students in Mainstream Classrooms." *The Reading Teacher* 54, no. 8 (2001): 750–57.

Blackline Masters

Unpunctuated Nonfiction Passage (1)

Wolves do not talk like we do but they communicate in other ways they make many sounds including whimpers growls barks whines and pants all of which mean different things a growl means a wolf is not happy and a whimper says that it is scared or hurt adult wolves hardly ever bark but pups bark when they are playing or to call for help a wolfs most famous sound is the howl.

— from *A Pack of Wolves*

Excerpt from *A Pack of Wolves* by Louise and Richard Spilsbury. Reprinted by permission of Harcourt Education.

Unpunctuated Nonfiction Passage (2)

There are other problems for these reptiles some turtle eggs are crushed by vehicles on beaches while others are eaten by dogs raccoons jaguars and snakes hatchlings get caught by birds crabs and fish and larger turtles are killed so that fancy items may be made from their shells.

— from *Into the Sea*

from *1-2-3 Draw Ocean Life* by Freddie Levin

Dolphin
(6 to 13 feet long)

A dolphin is not a fish. It is a mammal that lives in the ocean. Mammals give birth and nurse their babies. A dolphin uses its tail to swim. Playful, friendly dolphins come to the surface and breathe air through their blow holes. They communicate in a language of clicks and squeaks.

1   Look at the shapes and lines in the first drawing. Lightly sketch a small circle for the head. Draw a small eye. Start the dolphin's body with two curved lines.

2   Draw the dolphin's snout. It's called a 'beak.' Add a dorsal fin.

3   Draw two flippers. Using curved lines, add the tail.

4   Look at the final drawing. Erase extra sketch lines. Shade and color your dolphin.

from ***Doodle a Zoodle*** by Deborah Zemke

Doodle a Zoodle

What is a zoodle? A zoodle is a doodle, but what kind? Can you guess? A doodle of a hippo is a zoodle, but a rhino doodle is not. A cheetah's a zoodle, but not a leopard. A piggy's a zoodle, but not a pig. Raccoons, butterflies, gibbons, buzzards, and barracudas—they're all zoodles. If you guessed that they're animals, you're right. And if you guessed that they're animals with double letters in their names, then you're double right!

Lots of animals have two eyes, two ears, two wings, or two legs. Even four-legged animals have two front legs and two hind legs. Why so many twos? Symmetry! What's symmetry? Let's look at Molly, the border collie.

If we draw a line down the center, we see that Molly is the same on the left as on the right. Even her nose has two nostrils. That's symmetry!

Is Molly a zoodle? Absoloodle! Look for the two L's that started this doodle.

Doodle lines and shapes that you'll be using...

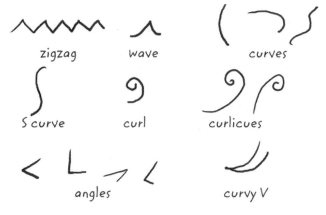

zigzag   wave   curves

S curve   curl   curlicues

angles   curvy V

Some shapes and lines that are especially useful for drawing zoodles:

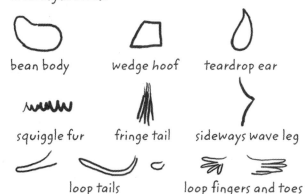

bean body   wedge hoof   teardrop ear

squiggle fur   fringe tail   sideways wave leg

loop tails   loop fingers and toes

Excerpt from *Doodle a Zoodle* ©2006 by Deborah Zemke. Used by permission of Chronicle Books LLC, San Francisco. Visit Chroniclebooks.com.

from **Doodle a Zoodle** by Deborah Zemke

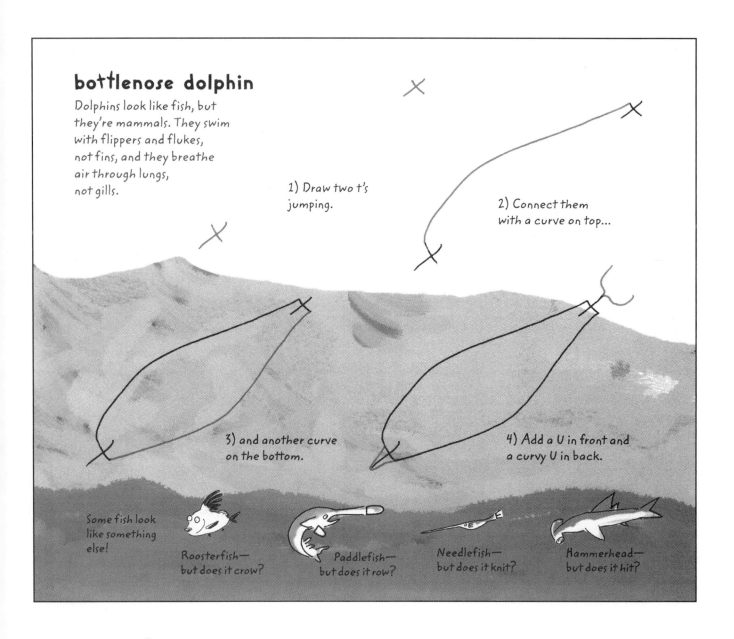

bottlenose dolphin

Dolphins look like fish, but they're mammals. They swim with flippers and flukes, not fins, and they breathe air through lungs, not gills.

1) Draw two t's jumping.

2) Connect them with a curve on top...

3) and another curve on the bottom.

4) Add a U in front and a curvy U in back.

Some fish look like something else!

Roosterfish— but does it crow?

Paddlefish— but does it row?

Needlefish— but does it knit?

Hammerhead— but does it hit?

from **_Doodle a Zoodle_** by Deborah Zemke

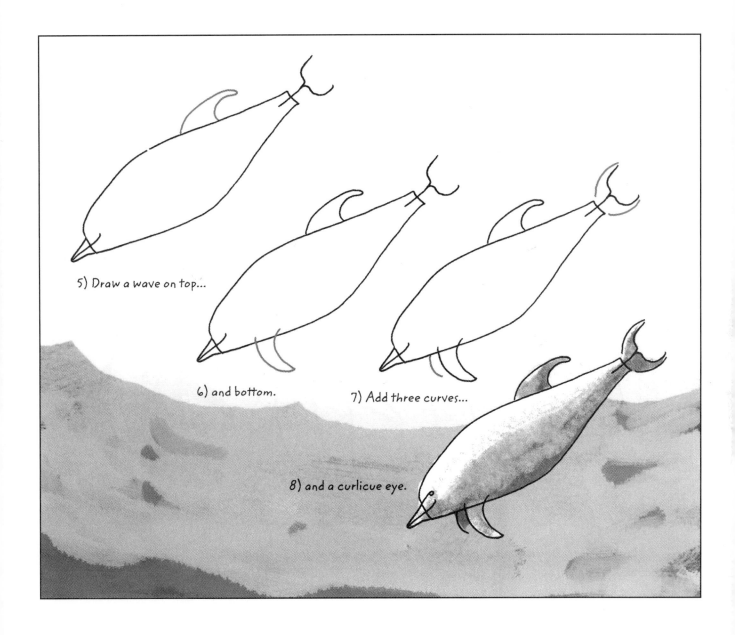

5) Draw a wave on top...

6) and bottom.

7) Add three curves...

8) and a curlicue eye.

from **Doodle a Zoodle** by Deborah Zemke

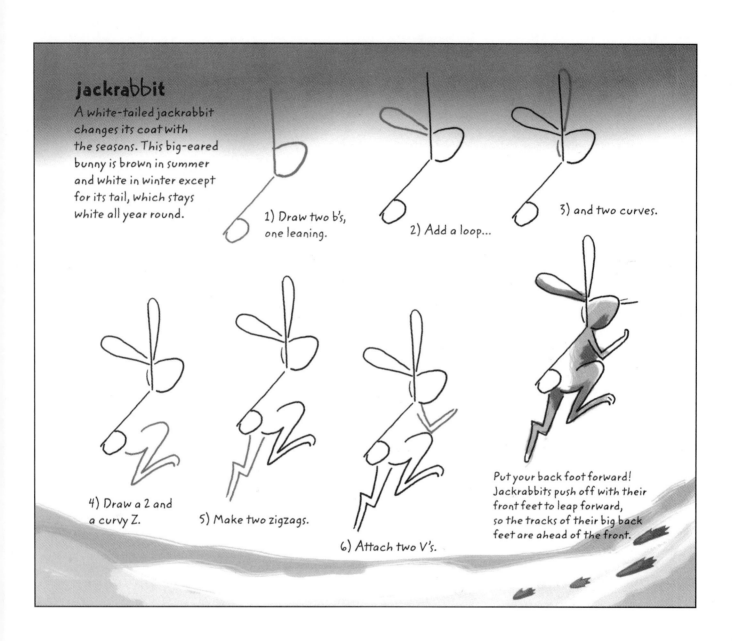

jackrabbit

A white-tailed jackrabbit changes its coat with the seasons. This big-eared bunny is brown in summer and white in winter except for its tail, which stays white all year round.

1) Draw two b's, one leaning.

2) Add a loop...

3) and two curves.

4) Draw a 2 and a curvy Z.

5) Make two zigzags.

6) Attach two V's.

Put your back foot forward! Jackrabbits push off with their front feet to leap forward, so the tracks of their big back feet are ahead of the front.

Excerpt from *Doodle a Zoodle* ©2006 by Deborah Zemke. Used by permission of Chronicle Books LLC, San Francisco. Visit Chroniclebooks.com.

Puzzle Sticks

Materials: craft sticks

1. Lay twelve craft sticks side by side. Line the ends up evenly. Tape the sticks to keep them lined up and then number them from one to twelve. Flip the sticks over.

2. Use a pencil to sketch a picture on the untaped side. Color the picture with markers. Remove the tape from the back.

3. Mix up the sticks and then try to put them back together. You can make a more difficult puzzle by using more sticks.

"Puzzle Sticks" from *Fun-To-Make Crafts for Every Day* ©2005 Boyds Mills Press. Reprinted with permission of Boyds Mills Press, Inc.

Putting on Your Shoes and Socks

1. Put on your right shoe.

2. Tie the laces on the left shoe.

3. Put on your left shoe.

4. Make the right shoe tight.

5. Put on your right sock.

Being a Writer™ Reorder Information

Grade 3

Additional Units

Poetry Genre Unit (Teacher's Manual and CD-ROM Reproducible Materials)	BWA-GU3-1
Letter Writing Genre Unit (Teacher's Manual, 2 trade books, and CD-ROM Reproducible Materials)	BWA-GU3-2
Additional Genre Units Package (Poetry Genre Unit and Letter Writing Genre Unit)	BWA-GUP3-1
Preparing for a Writing Test, Grades 3–5 (Teacher's Manual and CD-ROM Reproducible Materials)	BWA-PWT35

Classroom Package — **BW-CP3**

Contents: Teacher's Manual (2 volumes), Skill Practice Teaching Guide, Assessment Resource Book, 25 Student Writing Handbooks, 25 Student Skill Practice Books, and 33 trade books.

Available separately

Teacher's Manual, vol. 1	BW-TM3-V1
Teacher's Manual, vol. 2	BW-TM3-V2
Skill Practice Teaching Guide	BW-STG3
Assessment Resource Book	BW-AB3
Student Writing Handbook pack (5 books)	BW-SB3-Q5
Student Skill Practice Book pack (5 books)	BW-SSB3-Q5
CD-ROM Grade 3 Reproducible Materials	BW-CDR3
Trade book set (33 books)	BW-TBS3

Grade 4

Additional Units

Persuasive Nonfiction Genre Unit (Teacher's Manual and CD-ROM Reproducible Materials)	BWA-GU4-1
Letter Writing Genre Unit (Teacher's Manual and CD-ROM Reproducible Materials)	BWA-GU4-2
Additional Genre Units Package (Persuasive Nonfiction Genre Unit and Letter Writing Genre Unit)	BWA-GUP4-1
Preparing for a Writing Test, Grades 3–5 (Teacher's Manual and CD-ROM Reproducible Materials)	BWA-PWT35

Classroom Package — **BW-CP4**

Contents: Teacher's Manual (2 volumes), Skill Practice Teaching Guide, Assessment Resource Book, 30 Student Writing Handbooks, 30 Student Skill Practice Books, and 25 trade books.

Available separately

Teacher's Manual, vol. 1	BW-TM4-V1
Teacher's Manual, vol. 2	BW-TM4-V2
Skill Practice Teaching Guide	BW-STG4
Assessment Resource Book	BW-AB4
Student Writing Handbook pack (5 books)	BW-SB4-Q5
Student Skill Practice Book pack (5 books)	BW-SSB4-Q5
CD-ROM Grade 4 Reproducible Materials	BW-CDR4
Trade book set (25 books)	BW-TBS4

Grade 5

Additional Units

Letter Writing Genre Unit (Teacher's Manual, 1 trade book, and CD-ROM Reproducible Materials)	BWA-GU5-1
Functional Writing Genre Unit (Teacher's Manual and CD-ROM Reproducible Materials)	BWA-GU5-2
Additional Genre Units Package (Letter Writing Genre Unit and Functional Writing Genre Unit)	BWA-GUP5-1
Preparing for a Writing Test, Grades 3–5 (Teacher's Manual and CD-ROM Reproducible Materials)	BWA-PWT35

Classroom Package — **BW-CP5**

Contents: Teacher's Manual (2 volumes), Skill Practice Teaching Guide, Assessment Resource Book, 30 Student Writing Handbooks, 30 Student Skill Practice Books, and 25 trade books.

Available separately

Teacher's Manual, vol. 1	BW-TM5-V1
Teacher's Manual, vol. 2	BW-TM5-V2
Skill Practice Teaching Guide	BW-STG5
Assessment Resource Book	BW-AB5
Student Writing Handbook pack (5 books)	BW-SB5-Q5
Student Skill Practice Book pack (5 books)	BW-SSB5-Q5
CD-ROM Grade 5 Reproducible Materials	BW-CDR5
Trade book set (25 books)	BW-TBS5

Grade 6

Additional Units

Letter Writing Genre Unit (Teacher's Manual, 1 trade book, and CD-ROM Reproducible Materials)	BWA-GU6-1
Functional Writing Genre Unit (Teacher's Manual, 1 trade book, and CD-ROM Reproducible Materials)	BWA-GU6-2
Additional Genre Units Package (Letter Writing Genre Unit and Functional Writing Genre Unit)	BWA-GUP6-1

Classroom Package — **BW-CP6**

Contents: Teacher's Manual (2 volumes), Skill Practice Teaching Guide, Assessment Resource Book, 30 Student Writing Handbooks (2 volumes), 30 Student Skill Practice Books, and 14 trade books.

Available separately

Teacher's Manual, vol. 1	BW-TM6-V1
Teacher's Manual, vol. 2	BW-TM6-V2
Skill Practice Teaching Guide	BW-STG6
Assessment Resource Book	BW-AB6
Student Writing Handbook pack (5 books)	BW-SB6-Q5
Student Skill Practice Book pack (5 books)	BW-SSB6-Q5
CD-ROM Grade 6 Reproducible Materials	BW-CDR6
Trade book set (14 books)	BW-TBS6

The *Being a Writer* program is also available at grades K–2. Visit www.devstu.org for more information.

Ordering Information:

To order call 800.666.7270 * fax 510.842.0348 * log on to www.devstu.org * e-mail pubs@devstu.org

Or Mail Your Order to:

Developmental Studies Center * Publications Department * 2000 Embarcadero, Suite 305 * Oakland, CA 94606-5300

DEVELOPMENTAL STUDIES CENTER™